The Book of
Home
Sewing

DRS	
OO KEN	
LEA	
LIL	
MER	
WHI	

The Book of
Home
Sewing

Maggi McCormick Gordon

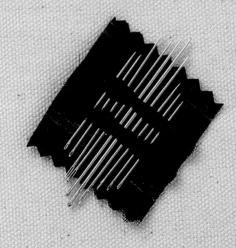

C&B

COLLINS & BROWN

First published in Great Britain in 1997 by
COLLINS & BROWN LIMITED
London House
Great Eastern Wharf
Parkgate Road
London SW11 4NQ

1 3 5 7 9 8 6 4 2

British Library Cataloguing-in-Publication Data:
A catalogue record for this book is available
from the British Library.

ISBN 1 85585 287 X (hardback)
ISBN 1 85585 670 0 (paperback)
Printed in Hong Kong by C&C Offset Printing Co., Ltd.

Editorial Director: Sarah Hoggett
Art Director: Roger Bristow
Project Editor: Lisa Dyer
Assistant Editor: Corinne Asghar
Senior Art Editor: Julia Ward-Hastelow
Designer: Liz Brown
Stitched samples: Doreen James
Photographer: Matthew Ward
Additional photography: Sampson Lloyd
Jacket photography: Geoff Dann
Illustrators: Amanda Patton, David Ashby
Index: Ingrid Lock

CONTENTS

DRESSMAKING 48

HOME FURNISHINGS 88

About This Book

THE BOOK OF HOME SEWING is a step-by-step guide to successful sewing for both complete beginners and those interested in improving their skills. The book begins with tools and equipment and other essentials, and guides you through the information required for any sewing task, from patterns and stitches to seams, gathers and bindings. The chapter on dressmaking looks at the component parts of garments – hems, collars, cuffs and so on – and takes you step by step through the process of making them. The section on altering patterns and existing garments shows how to ensure

Decorative Finishes

Creating your own unique designs is one of the most exciting aspects of sewing. This book includes imaginative and attractive ways of making your projects unique.

Making and Adapting

All the information needed to make a typical garment is contained in Getting Started, Sewing Basics and Dressmaking.

Dressmaking

By following the step-by-step illustrations, you will be able to assemble and finish virtually any straightforward garment.

Page Layout

Each double-page spread has been carefully designed to give the reader comprehensive but concise information about each technique or method. The arrangement of the pages provides quick, visual access, with full-color photographs and artwork to illustrate each step.

Introduction

Each section has a clear heading and an introduction that contains informative general data about the techniques outlined in the step-by-step text.

Variation

A purple border indicates information about alternative ways of carrying out a technique or method.

THE BOOK OF HOME SEWING

Hems

HEMS ARE USED TO FINISH THE BOTTOM of garments and the edges of simple sleeves, as well as the edges of such home furnishings as tablecloths, bedspreads and curtains. There are several methods for working hems, depending on the style of the garment or furnishing accessory, the weight of the fabric and the desired look.

Hems can be worked by hand or stitched on the machine, and in most cases should be virtually invisible. The usual way of making a hem is to turn under a narrow edge, and then turn the edge under again to enclose the raw edge completely. On heavyweight fabrics, or where there is not enough fabric to turn a hem, the edge can be faced or bound. All hems can be basted in place to help ensure accuracy, but pinning is usually enough.

Simple Hand-stitched Hem

1 Mark top and bottom of the hem by folding and pressing the fabric, and baste along the bottom foldline. Trim raw edge to ¼ in (5 mm) of the first fold.

2 Turn up and press the bottom foldline. Baste along the top marked line and through the center of the turned-up fold, making sure all seams match.

3 Turn under the top fold along the basted line and pin the hem in place. You can now sew the hem.

4 To work a tailor's hem, place the fabric wrong side up on a flat surface. Pick up 1 or 2 threads at a time while taking the needle through the edge of the top fold, removing pins as you work. When hemming is completed, remove all basting stitches.

TYPES OF HAND-SEWN HEMS

There are many ways of working a hand-sewn hem, and you may like to experiment with a few different techniques to decide which one you prefer.

Bias or straight binding is machine-stitched to the raw edge of a levelled hem, then turned up and pressed, and then hand- or machine-stitched in place.

The raw edge is zigzagged, then turned up. The hem is herringbone-stitched in place.

On lightweight fabric, the raw edge is turned under and machine-stitched, folded up and basted, and then sewn with a tailor's hem, as described in step 4 above.

Fusible hem tape is good for emergency repairs and can be used on lightweight fabrics, though it may work loose during laundering. Here the raw edge has been pinked and turned up, and the tape inserted into the fold and pressed in place.

any pattern fits perfectly and suggests ways of putting new life into outmoded or outgrown clothes.

The Home Furnishings chapter includes bedlinen, table linen, curtains, cushions and covers, and contains ideas that will add flair to your living spaces.

The final chapter looks at care and repair, including mending, stain removal, and a guide to laundry and cleaning symbols.

Imperial and metric measurements have been used throughout. As conversions are not precise, you should use either one system or the other consistently.

Home Furnishing Made Simple
The chapter on home furnishings leads you step by step to success, from making your own duvets and pillow cases to covering a sofa and making cushions and curtains to match.

DRESSMAKING • Hems

HAND STITCHES

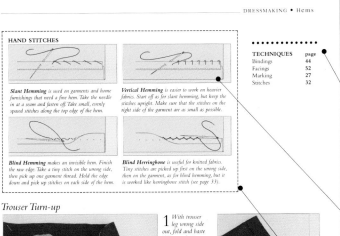

Slant Hemming is used on garments and home furnishings that need a fine hem. Take the needle in at a seam and fasten off. Take small, evenly spaced stitches along the top edge of the hem.

Vertical Hemming is easier to work on heavier fabrics. Start off as for slant hemming, but keep the stitches upright. Make sure that the stitches on the right side of the garment are as small as possible.

Blind Hemming makes an invisible hem. Finish the raw edge. Take a tiny stitch on the wrong side, then pick up one garment thread. Hold the edge down and pick up stitches on each side of the hem.

Blind Herringbone is useful for knitted fabrics. Tiny stitches are picked up first on the wrong side, then on the garment, as for blind hemming, but it is worked like herringbone stitch (see page 33).

TECHNIQUES	page
Bindings	44
Facings	52
Marking	27
Stitches	32

Cross References
Yellow boxes in each section give a quick reference to related techniques throughout the book.

Illustrations
High-quality artwork illustrations are provided where it is clearer to see a technique in diagrammatic form.

Trouser Turn-up

1 With trouser leg wrong side out, fold and baste 3 lines – bottom edge of turn-up (bottom line), top of turn-up (center line), and trouser hemline (top line). Zigzag raw edge. Turn up the center fold and press. Secure zigzagged raw edge with herringbone stitch.

2 Turn trouser leg right side out. Turn up bottom fold and press. Turn under top fold and press. Catchstitch at the seams to secure. Remove the basting.

Useful Tips
A dotted border indicates useful hints and tricks of the trade that make a technique clearer or easier to carry out.

Curved Hem

1 Carefully mark and cut the hem. Zigzag the raw edge and baste the foldline. Run a row of gathering stitches 1/4 in (5 mm) from the zigzagging.

2 Turn up the hem along the tacked foldline. Baste the hem in place about 1/4 in (5 mm) from the fold.

3 Matching the seams, pin the hem in place, pulling up the gathering thread as you work to spread the fabric evenly and ease in fullness.

4 Herringbone-stitch the hem in place from the wrong side, removing pins as you work. Remove all basting and press.

65

Step-by-steps
Easy-to-follow photographs are used to illustrate each technique clearly. Most of the stitching is worked in a contrasting color for clarity.

New Ideas
New approaches to making home furnishings and finishing garments will spark off a host of ideas that will have you itching to stitch.

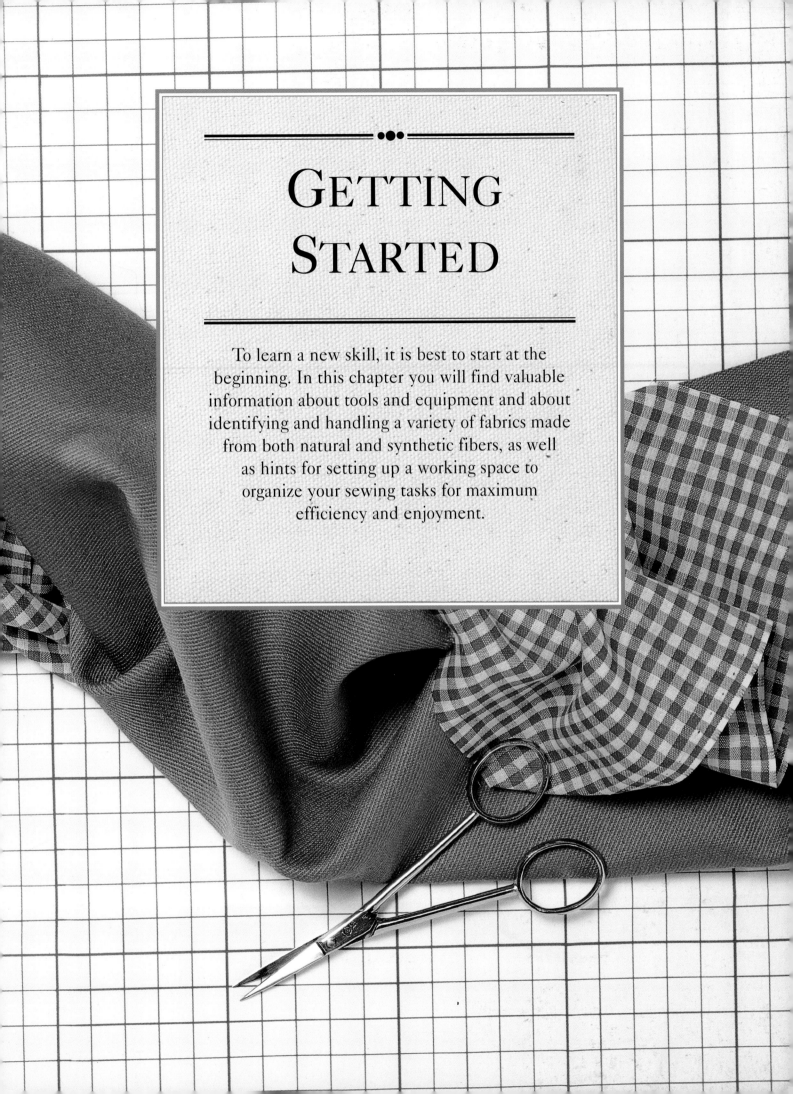

GETTING STARTED

To learn a new skill, it is best to start at the beginning. In this chapter you will find valuable information about tools and equipment and about identifying and handling a variety of fabrics made from both natural and synthetic fibers, as well as hints for setting up a working space to organize your sewing tasks for maximum efficiency and enjoyment.

Tools and Equipment

YOU WILL NOT NEED all the items shown here for basic sewing projects, and there are other tools that you may prefer to use. Basic items to have in stock are hand-sewing needles, straight pins, a tape measure and a ruler, some marking tools, dressmaker's shears and smaller sewing scissors, and an iron and ironing board.

Measuring and Marking Tools

A flexible tape measure is essential for taking body measurements and measuring objects such as sofas and chairs. Rigid rulers and T-squares are useful for measuring on a hard work surface. Carbon and a tracing wheel are used to transfer markings from a pattern to fabric. Colored chalks, pencils or fabric markers are handy for more approximate markings, such as to mark hems, but can also be used in conjunction with a ruler for marking straight edges. For more information on marking, see page 27.

Pins, Needles and Thread

Use straight stainless-steel pins for most general purposes. You can also buy special-purpose pins, such as T-pins for heavyweight fabrics and lace pins for delicates. As regards needles, 'sharps' are the best for general use. 'Betweens' are good for heavier fabrics. Darning and upholstery needles are also available, as well as those for needlecraft use. Make sure your needle glides easily through the fabric, otherwise the fabric fibers may be damaged. Basting thread is a soft, loose cotton thread, available in black and white and is easy to remove from fabric. For information on other threads, see page 13.

Sewing Aids

Pincushions, thimbles and needle threaders are not essential, but all make sewing easier. Bodkins can be used to thread elastic through casings, as well as to tease out sharp corners on collars.

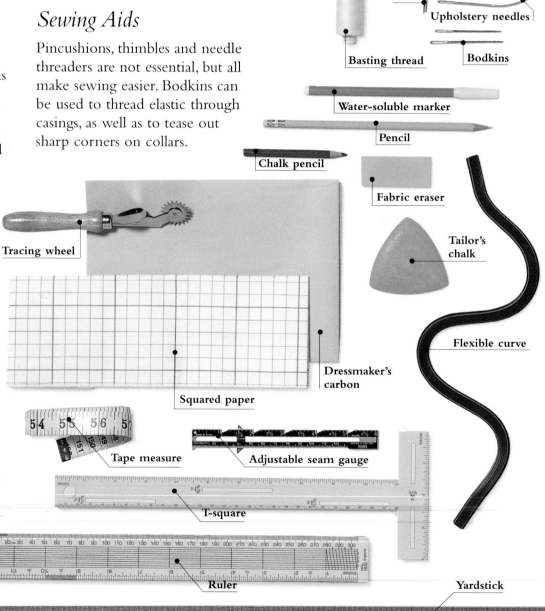

Pincushion

Needle threader

Needles

Thimble

Pins

Upholstery needles

Basting thread

Bodkins

Water-soluble marker

Pencil

Chalk pencil

Fabric eraser

Tailor's chalk

Tracing wheel

Flexible curve

Squared paper

Dressmaker's carbon

Tape measure

Adjustable seam gauge

T-square

Ruler

Yardstick

10 millimetres (mm) = 1 centimetre (cm)   100 centimetres (cm)

Cutting Tools

You should never use fabric-cutting scissors on paper or batting (wadding); both dull the blades and will eventually ruin them.

A good pair of dressmaker's shears with bent handles is essential for cutting out patterns. Small sewing or embroidery scissors are essential for more detailed work, such as clipping and trimming seams. Pinking shears are excellent for finishing seams (see page 38). A seam ripper is easier to use than scissors for removing stitches (see page 156).

Pressing

A steam iron and an ironing surface are essential pieces of sewing equipment (see page 40). A tailor's ham is useful for pressing awkward areas, such as darts and curved seams. A sleeveboard is placed inside sleeves so they can be pressed without causing any unwanted creasing.

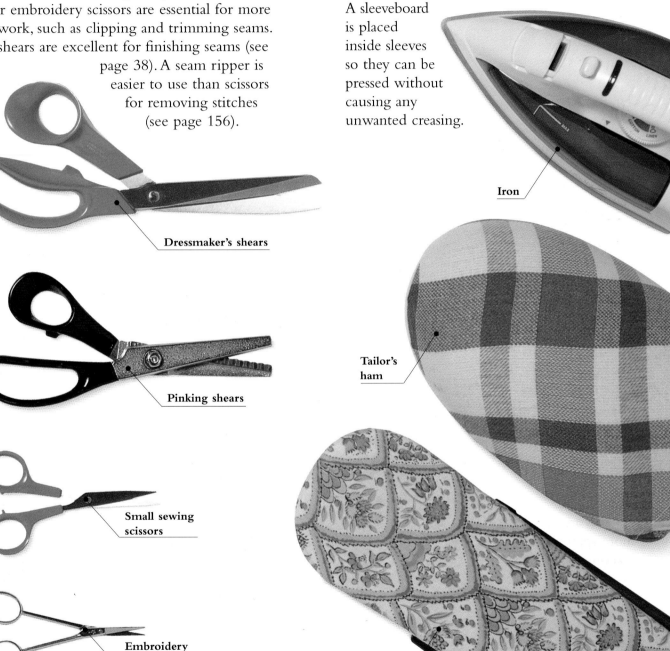

Dressmaker's shears

Pinking shears

Small sewing scissors

Embroidery scissors

Seam ripper

Iron

Tailor's ham

Sleeveboard

1 metre (m)   1000 metres (m)   =   1 kilometre (km)

Natural Fabrics

FABRIC IS THE MEDIUM in which the dressmaker creates. The choices available are staggering and can be confusing. To produce a garment or furnishing that you are happy with, you must choose the right fabric for the design. The best way to learn about fabric is to work with it, but get to know it first by examining and touching it. Visit fabric shops and the fabric department of large stores, and handle fabrics that appeal to you – the feel of a fabric is one of its most important qualities.

Natural fabrics are those made from natural fibers: cotton, linen, wool and silk. Each type has many variations in weight, weave and use.

Silk

Silk is woven from long filaments produced by silkworms. So valued was silk in Ancient China that its manufacture was a closely guarded secret until a number of silkworm cocoons and mulberry tree seeds (the silkworm's only food) were smuggled to the Middle East.

Silk is strong and can be woven into an enormous variety of weights and weaves, from gossamer sheers to heavy slubbed upholstery fabrics. Some silks can be hand-washed or machine-washed, but most must be dry-cleaned.

Wool

Warm and absorbent, wool is produced in a variety of weights and weaves, and woven or knitted.

Wool for home-sewing use varies from lightweight Viyella® (actually a 55% wool, 45% cotton blend) to gabardine for suits and jackets. Wool fleece can be used to line coats, while mohair and angora are luxurious, long-fibered wools for knitted and woven garments. Some wools can be washed by hand, but most need to be dry-cleaned.

Viyella®

Worsted

Gauze (butter muslin)

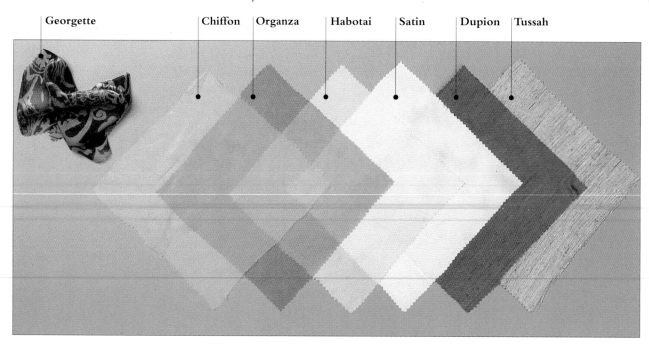

Georgette | Chiffon | Organza | Habotai | Satin | Dupion | Tussah

Suit-weight
wool

Coat-weight
wool

Linen

Linen is the fiber of the flax
plant. Its texture varies from a
smooth finish to a rough
slub, and it can be woven
into such diverse
fabrics as fine cloth
used for handkerchiefs,
highly absorbent
towelling, garment-weight
fabrics, and even heavy canvas.

Linen is cool to wear and has a
wonderful characteristic strength and
luster, but pure linen creases easily. This
crumpled look has a certain fashion value, but is not
always desirable, so many linen fabrics used for
dressmaking are blended with synthetic fibers to help
them hold their shape.

Linen

Cheesecloth

Madras

Printed cotton

Masouk

Shirt-weight
cotton

Muslin
(calico)

Drill

Velvet

Cotton

Cotton is made from the fibers of the cotton plant. It takes
many forms, from sheer Gauze (butter muslin) and
lightweight lawn to thick, sturdy corduroy and denim.
Cotton takes dye well and is easy to launder. It can be
woven into such patterns as plaids, or designs can be stamped
on it after weaving. As a knit, it is soft, supple and hangs and
washes well. It is often blended with synthetic fibers,
especially in permanent-press fabrics (see pages 14-15).

CHOOSING THREAD From left to right:
Thread comes in a variety of cotton, polyester
weights and can be made and sewing silk
from several fibers. Cotton
and polyester, often combined,
are generally used for home
sewing and dressmaking.
Sewing silk is more expensive
and difficult to work with,
but is sometimes used
with finer fabrics.

Man-made Fabrics

THE VARIETY OF MAN-MADE, synthetic fibers available is so broad that no attempt can be made to describe them specifically. They include acetate, acrylic, polyester, nylon and rayon. While many fabrics are 100% synthetic, many are blended with natural fibers (see pages 12–13) to amalgamate the best features of each type and to make them less expensive.

Most synthetic fabrics, and many blends, fray easily. Use very sharp scissors to cut the fabric, and leave a generous seam allowance to overcome the potential problem.

One of the main characteristics of man-made fabrics is that they are shrink- and crease-resistant. Most are also washable, and need little ironing if the care instructions are followed. Always use a cool iron when pressing, as all man-made fabrics scorch easily.

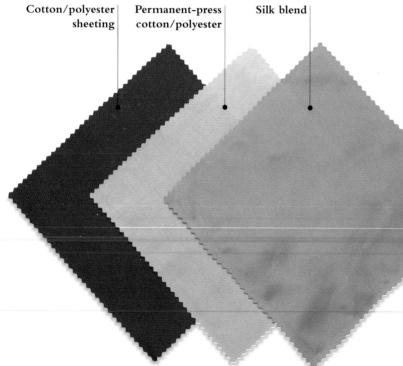

Woven velvet | Knitted velvet | Moiré taffeta

Synthetics

Most 100% synthetics have a silky quality. They fray easily, but are usually washable and hold their shape and body well. Although they can be hot to wear, the better-quality examples are virtually indistinguishable from silk, and less expensive.

Cotton/polyester sheeting | Permanent-press cotton/polyester | Silk blend

Blends

A huge selection of blended fabrics, made from a synthetic (usually polyester) mixed with a natural fiber (usually cotton), is available. Blended fabrics are available in a rainbow of plain colors, woven in patterns, or printed with small, medium or large patterns. They can be light-, medium- or heavyweight and are less likely to fray than 100% synthetics. Most wash-and-wear or permanent-press fabrics are blends, and therefore should be pressed with a cool iron only.

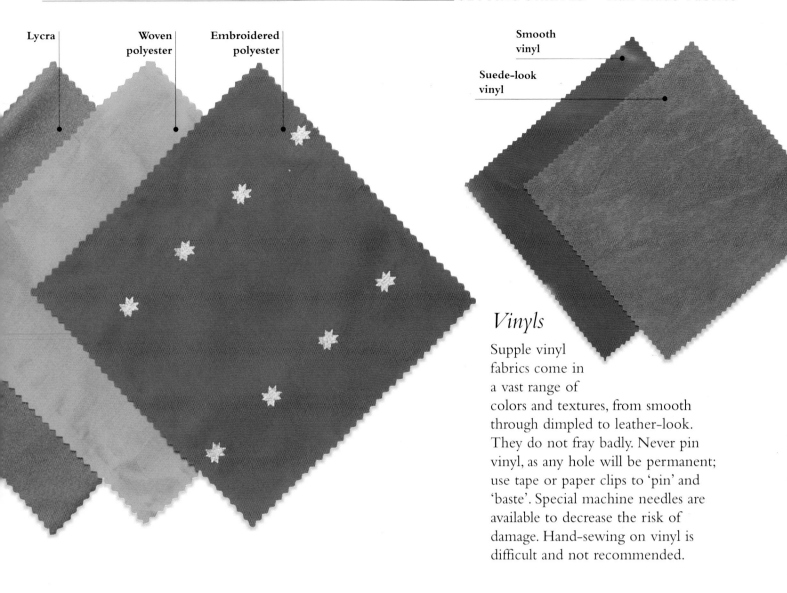

Lycra

Woven polyester

Embroidered polyester

Smooth vinyl

Suede-look vinyl

Vinyls

Supple vinyl fabrics come in a vast range of colors and textures, from smooth through dimpled to leather-look. They do not fray badly. Never pin vinyl, as any hole will be permanent; use tape or paper clips to 'pin' and 'baste'. Special machine needles are available to decrease the risk of damage. Hand-sewing on vinyl is difficult and not recommended.

Synthetic Sheers

The array of romantic-looking sheer fabrics available is due almost entirely to the advent of synthetic fibers. These fabrics are slippery, fray easily and are generally difficult to work with. They must be handled with care, given extra-wide seam allowances, pressed gently with a cool iron and basted at every stage.

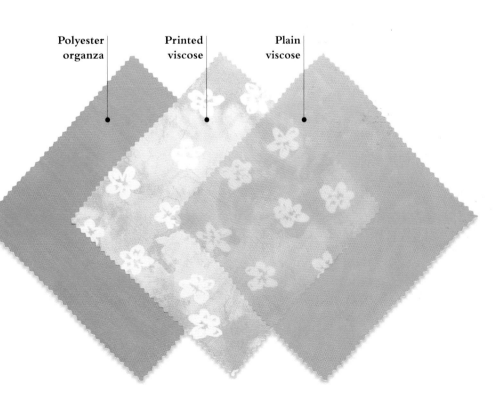

Polyester organza

Printed viscose

Plain viscose

Difficult Fabrics

MOST FABRICS WOVEN FROM SYNTHETIC or man-made fibers require a certain amount of special handling (see pages 14–15). The fabrics shown here and on the two following pages, though not all man made, are all difficult to work with and need special care both in cutting and stitching and as finished garments. However, items made from these fabrics are usually special-occasion wear that can be well worth the extra attention they require.

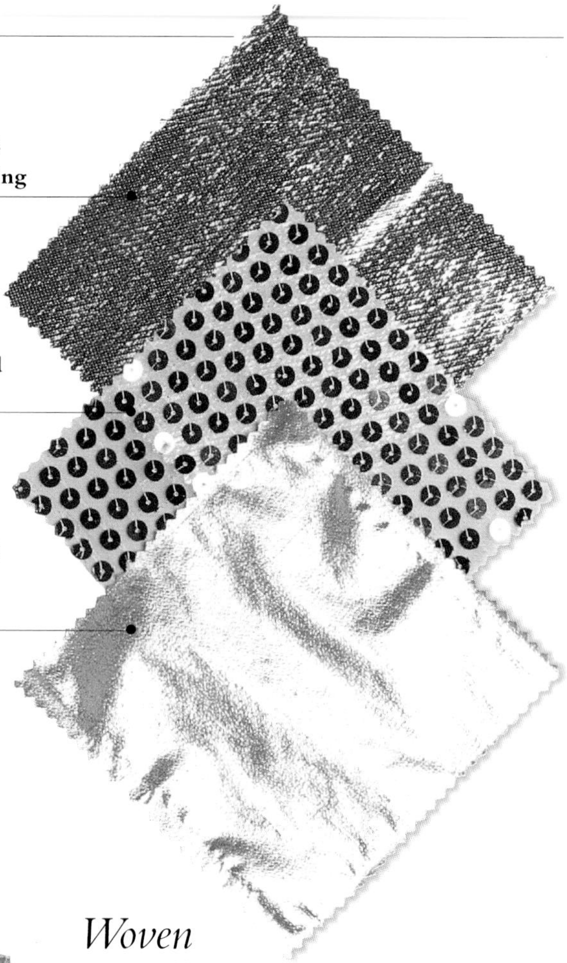

Gold lamé with backing

Sequinned fabric

Gold lamé without backing

Fake snakeskin

Pinwale corduroy

Woven cotton velvet

Two-tone velvet

Fake fur

Woven Metallics

Metallic thread has been used to weave the two lamé fabrics; both fray very easily. For the sequinned fabric, individual sequins have been stitched to a sheer woven backing fabric at regular intervals; try not to cut through sequins and avoid structured garments with darts.

Napped Fabrics

Fabrics with a nap or pile must be cut out with the pile running in the same direction on all pieces. Because these fabrics tend to be thick, you should aim for simple designs with few darts, gathers or pleats. Use fine pins and needles and baste everything before stitching.

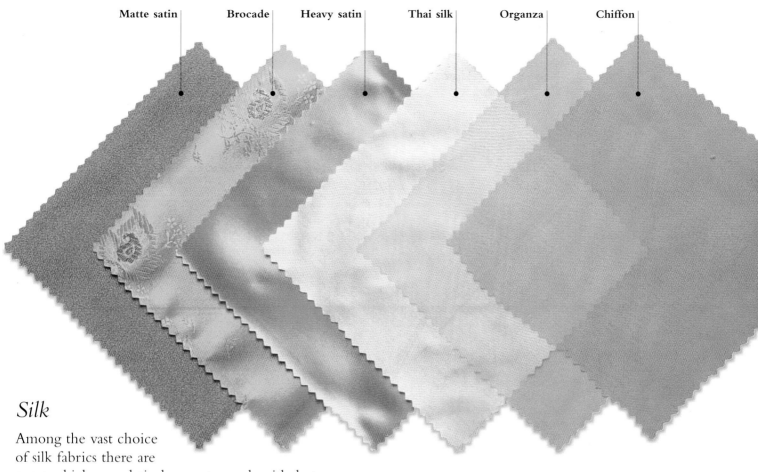

Matte satin | Brocade | Heavy satin | Thai silk | Organza | Chiffon

Silk

Among the vast choice
of silk fabrics there are
some which are relatively easy to work with, but
most should be considered difficult. Many silks,
and their synthetic cousins, fray easily, and all are
slippery to handle. Use fine pins and needles, cut
extra-wide seam allowances, and baste everything.
Press on the wrong side with a cool iron, using a
pressing cloth or brown paper to protect the fabric.

Lace and Net

Lace and net fabrics are machine-made in a huge
variety of weights and designs. Unless they are
made into a sheer overgarment, they need to be
lined. This adds support to the fabric's structure
and keeps it from scratching. Always cut the
fabric so the design runs in the same direction.

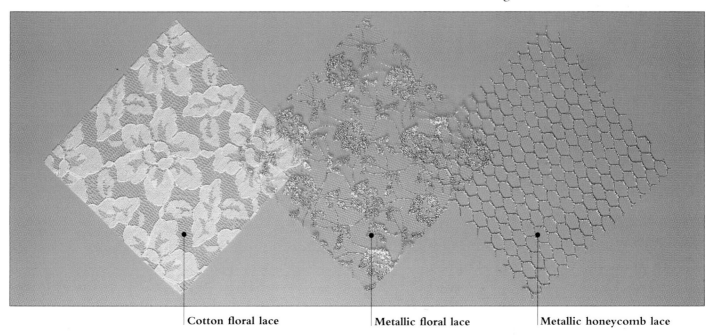

Cotton floral lace | Metallic floral lace | Metallic honeycomb lace

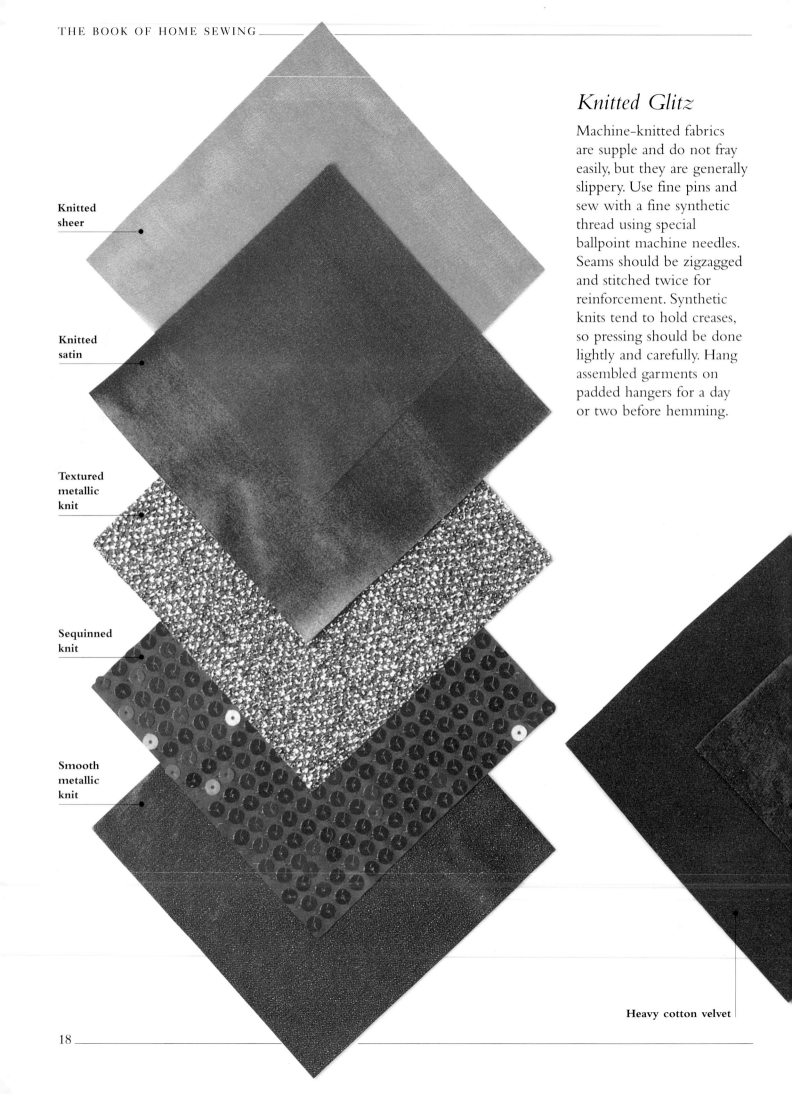

Knitted sheer

Knitted satin

Textured metallic knit

Sequinned knit

Smooth metallic knit

Knitted Glitz

Machine-knitted fabrics are supple and do not fray easily, but they are generally slippery. Use fine pins and sew with a fine synthetic thread using special ballpoint machine needles. Seams should be zigzagged and stitched twice for reinforcement. Synthetic knits tend to hold creases, so pressing should be done lightly and carefully. Hang assembled garments on padded hangers for a day or two before hemming.

Heavy cotton velvet

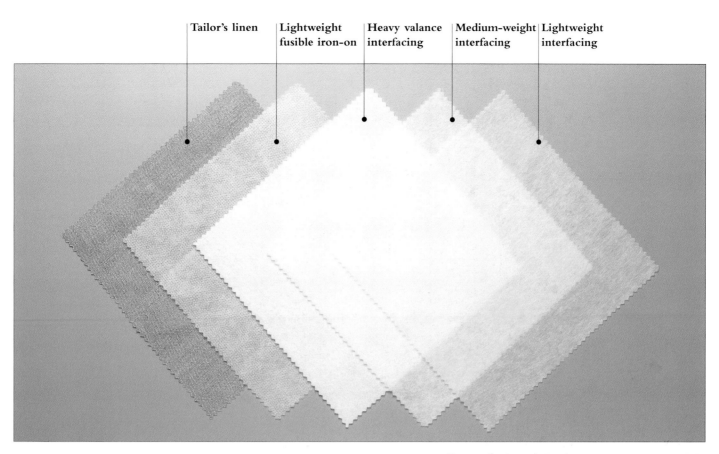

Tailor's linen | Lightweight fusible iron-on | Heavy valance interfacing | Medium-weight interfacing | Lightweight interfacing

Long-pile synthetic velvet | Short-pile synthetic velvet

Interfacing

An interfacing is a separate piece of fabric inserted between the garment piece and its facing to add strength and stability. The type – woven or non-woven, sew-in or fusible – and the weight, varying from light to heavy, are determined by the garment fabric. The pattern will specify which pieces need to be interfaced.

Velvet Knits

Knitted velvet is softer and more supple than its woven counterpart, and it frays less easily. Treat as a napped fabric (see page 16), cutting out pattern pieces with the pile running in the same direction (upward if possible). It is advisable to stitch darts and seams in the direction of the pile, and to insert zippers by hand. Finish seam allowances by hand or machine to prevent stretching, and apply hem tape or bias binding to hem edges. Avoid using buttonholes if possible; substitute loops or hidden fastenings.

Workroom Knowhow

A NEAT, TIDY WORKING space can make the difference between enjoying the time spent sewing and finding sewing a chore. Everyday objects such as empty shoeboxes can be recycled and labelled to make excellent storage containers. With a little planning and foresight, and by working tidily, you can maximize the time you have to sew.

Organizing a Room

If you are lucky enough to have an extra room to devote to sewing, you will want to use it to its full potential. Alternatively, a spare bedroom or study can do double duty; use a desk as the sewing machine table. The essential requirements for any sewing area are a sewing table; deep shelves, cupboards or drawers for storing fabrics and boxes of tools; and bookshelf space. You will also need a large table for cutting fabric. A folding house-decorator's table is ideal if you have space to store it; otherwise, a dining-room table can be used. The iron and ironing board do not need to be stored in the sewing room, but must be easily accessible. A pinboard is handy to have nearby, and a full-length mirror is useful for dressmaking. Adequate electrical outlets and good lighting are essential.

Storing Small Items

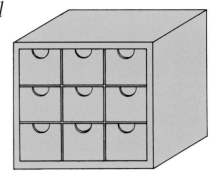

A ready-made tool box or hardware unit, shown here, is useful for storing small items such as threads, pins and needles. Clear plastic drawers enable you to see at a glance what is stored in each drawer. Otherwise, label each drawer.

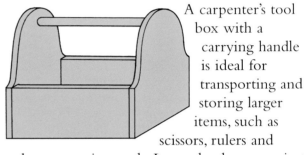

A carpenter's tool box with a carrying handle is ideal for transporting and storing larger items, such as scissors, rulers and other measuring tools. Large shoeboxes are just the right size for filing pattern envelopes.

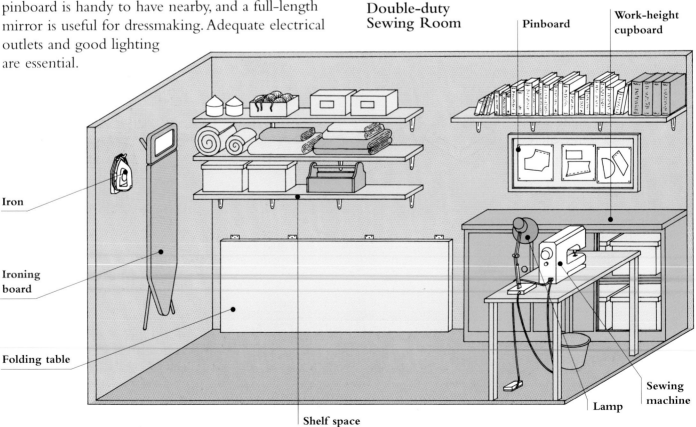

Double-duty Sewing Room

Pinboard

Work-height cupboard

Iron

Ironing board

Folding table

Shelf space

Lamp

Sewing machine

Small Spaces

If you do not have a spare room, convert a small unused space, such as the area under the stairs, into a workroom. Set up a sewing table at the high end and have storage shelves built into the low end. A door will help keep bolts of fabric and materials clean. An iron, ironing board and pinboard can be hung on hooks on a partition wall or behind the sewing table, and more shelves can be put up above them.

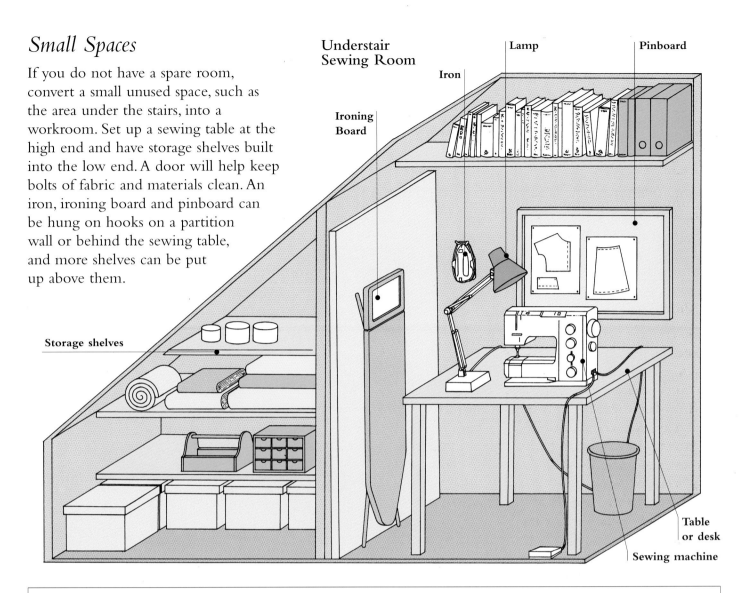

Understair Sewing Room

Iron

Lamp

Pinboard

Ironing Board

Storage shelves

Table or desk

Sewing machine

Working

Wherever you work, make sure that your table and chair are at a comfortable height. Keep all electrical wires safely out of the way. Turn off the machine if leaving it for any length of time. Keep all frequently used tools and equipment handy so you don't have to get up every time you need them. Finally, remember that sewing for long stretches is tiring – take regular breaks and stand up and move around.

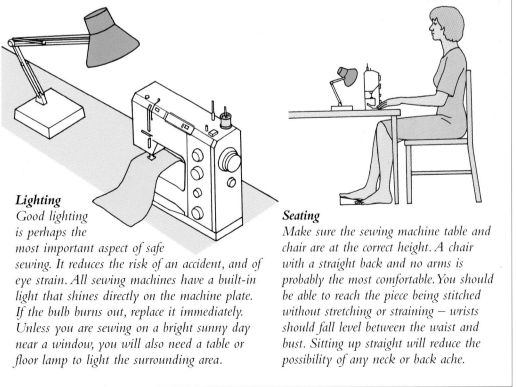

Lighting
Good lighting is perhaps the most important aspect of safe sewing. It reduces the risk of an accident, and of eye strain. All sewing machines have a built-in light that shines directly on the machine plate. If the bulb burns out, replace it immediately. Unless you are sewing on a bright sunny day near a window, you will also need a table or floor lamp to light the surrounding area.

Seating
Make sure the sewing machine table and chair are at the correct height. A chair with a straight back and no arms is probably the most comfortable. You should be able to reach the piece being stitched without stretching or straining – wrists should fall level between the waist and bust. Sitting up straight will reduce the possibility of any neck or back ache.

SEWING BASICS

This chapter is all about understanding: understanding patterns, fabrics and your sewing machine; understanding how to work a wide variety of stitches and seams and how to use them to the best advantage; understanding the general techniques inherent in all sewing, such as pressing versus ironing, mitering, pleats and gathers, and borders and bindings.

Understanding Patterns

OCCASIONALLY WE HEAR OF PEOPLE, usually famous couture designers, who do not need to cut a pattern. They drape the fabric here, pin it there and, with a few snips of the scissors, can run up an outfit to die for. Most of us lack either the skill or confidence to work without a pattern, either a commercial pattern or one that we have designed and cut ourselves.

For those starting out in dressmaking, it is advisable to use a commercial pattern until you have more experience in how a garment is put together and understand the technical aspects of the craft.

Measuring the Body

Before purchasing a pattern, you need to know what size to buy. Commercial patterns are clearly marked with the measurements of certain crucial body dimensions, and these determine the size. Use a tape measure to take all the body measurements shown in the diagrams below. Keep a note of all the measurements handy when shopping for a pattern, as standard measurements may vary between pattern manufacturers.

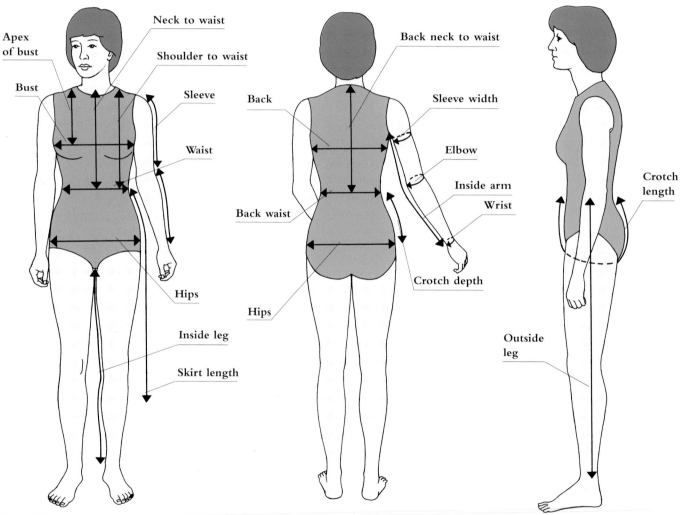

Front View
Certain measurements, such as the bust and apex of bust, can only be measured from the front. Those that encircle the body, such as waist and hips, are taken from the front and the back. Sleeve length should be measured along the outside of the arm.

Back View
Most standard measurements taken from the back are simply continuations of encircling ones, but those such as neck to waist or width of back may be important for altering a pattern later (see page 82).

Side View
The outside leg is the most important side-view measurement, and should be taken from the waist to the finished length of trousers. The crotch length should be comfortable: not too tight, but not too loose.

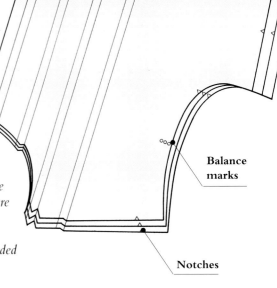

Using Paper Patterns

Pattern manufacturers publish seasonal catalogs with photographs and drawings of each garment or craft project available. These pattern books are displayed in fabric shops and departments, and customers select patterns from them.

The sizes are based on average statistics, which are compiled regularly and represent an idealized, rather than a completely realistic, figure. Commercial patterns are marked so that alterations can be made to fit your individual measurements. Before laying out the pattern and cutting the fabric, check your body measurements against the pattern and make any alterations necessary (see pages 82–5). Make a thorough check before beginning work on any new garment.

Sizes and Symbols
Commercial patterns are multi-sized; that is, they are marked with coded cutting lines for three or four different sizes. Be very careful in cutting out to follow the line marked for your size. Most patterns are printed in several languages, but the symbols used are fairly standard (see page 26). Always check the key provided on the pattern envelope.

Balance marks

Notches

MATCHING PATTERNS

Fabric patterns, such as plaids, checks and stripes, should match in order to give a professional-looking finish to a garment. With vertical stripes, as here, careful positioning of the shoulder seams means that the pattern will match. If the stripes run horizontally on the fabric, match from the waist seam upward; the bust dart will throw the alignment off, but this area will be concealed under the arm. When calculating the amount of fabric required, always allow a little extra fabric for matching patterns.

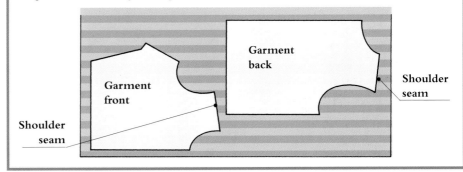

Garment front

Garment back

Shoulder seam

Shoulder seam

Planning a Pattern

First study the instruction sheet that comes with the pattern, which will give suggested layouts for pinning the pattern to the fabric. They have been worked out to make best use of the fabric width and to take account of fabrics that have a nap or pile (see pages 16 and 29). Different shading usually indicates the right and wrong sides of the fabric, lining and interfacing.

When you understand the layout, place the fabric on the work surface, folded with wrong sides together unless instructed otherwise. Arrange the pattern pieces on the fabric as shown, making sure they all fit before you begin to pin.

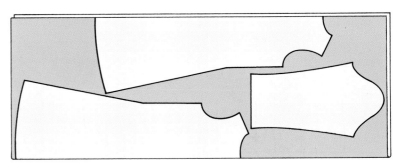

The pattern layout for the width of your fabric usually has all the pieces lying in the same direction so that fabrics with a distinctive print or grain will run the same way in the finished garment. A layout for 45-in (115-cm) wide fabric is shown above; a layout for 36-in (90-cm) wide fabric is shown below.

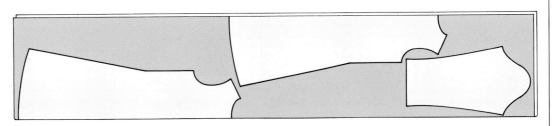

Pattern Symbols

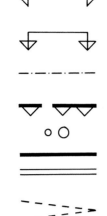

Pattern manufacturers use a variety of symbols. Most are universally understood, and all should be detailed in the instruction sheet or the pattern envelope.

Grain line
Place on straight grain of fabric, parallel to selvedge

Foldline
Place on fold of fabric

Center line
Center marking of front or back of garment

Notches and Dots
Locator marks for matching points on fabric

Cutting line

Adjustment lines
For lengthening or shortening garment

Dart line
Dotted line indicates edges to be joined

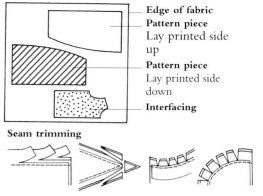

Edge of fabric
Pattern piece
Lay printed side up
Pattern piece
Lay printed side down
Interfacing

Seam trimming

Trim enclosed seams into layers

Trim corners

Clip inside curves

Notch outside curves

Pinning and Cutting

Take care when handling the pattern to avoid tearing the delicate tissue paper. Every pattern contains a variety of markings, most in the form of symbols (see above) to help you follow the instructions included with the pattern. Some, such as notches, are cut into the fabric when cutting out the pattern, but others must be transferred onto the fabric (see page 27).

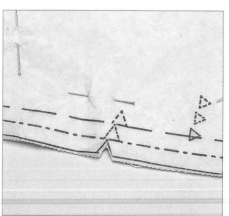

1 *Cut out each piece of the pattern from the paper sheet supplied, but do not cut away the excess paper at this stage. Using the lowest temperature setting on an iron, press each pattern piece carefully to eliminate creases.*

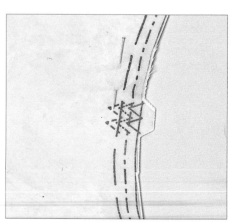

2 *Pin each pattern piece to the fabric following the cutting layout provided for the size, type and width of fabric. Pay close attention to the pattern markings to avoid wasteful mistakes.*

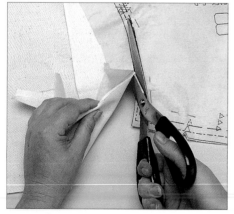

3 *Following the cutting line for the appropriate size, carefully cut out each piece of the pattern and discard the excess paper. Use sharp dressmaker's shears only — blunt household or paper scissors may fray or tear the fabric.*

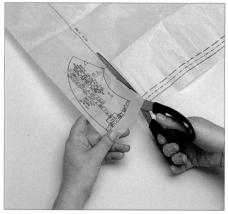

4 *Notches are used to mark matching points in the seamline. They may be arranged singly or in groups of two or three. Since they will be hidden in the seam, they can be cut into the seam allowance as shown.*

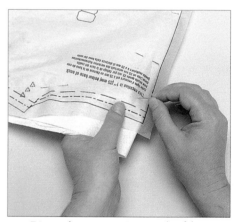

5 *This double notch has been cut outward, which some dressmakers prefer, especially on fabrics that are prone to fraying. To make cutting easier, cut the double notch as one unit, not two separate triangles. Single notches can also be cut outward, if preferred.*

MARKING FROM PATTERNS

Many marks on patterns relate to positioning the pattern on the fabric and cutting out, but some need to be transferred directly onto the fabric before the pattern is removed to be used as stitching guidelines or reference points for matching pieces together. Before unpinning the pattern from the fabric, always check that all marks have been transferred.

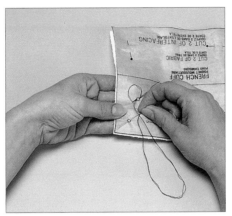

Water-Soluble Marker

Straight guidelines, such as pleats and tucks, can be marked using a ruler and a water-soluble marker pen. Fold back the pattern along the line to be marked and position the ruler along the edge. Mark a dotted or dashed line. The marks can be removed by steaming or dampening with water, or simply left in until the garment is laundered. This method is not suitable for use on fabrics that cannot be washed.

Tailor's Chalk

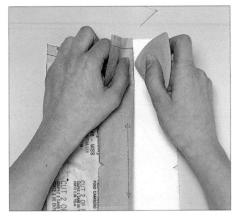

Tailor's chalk is available in a variety of colors, so choose one that will be visible on the color of fabric you are using. It can be brushed off nonwashable fabrics. To use, remove some pins and fold the unpinned section back to the point to be marked.

Tailor's Tacks

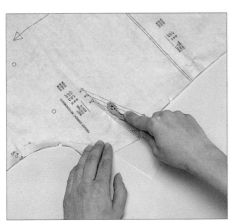

1 *Tailor's tacks are useful for button positions and balance marks. With the pattern pinned in place and a double length of thread, take a stitch through all layers. Take another stitch in the same spot and pull the thread to make a loop. Repeat as necessary.*

2 *When all the marks have been transferred, unpin the pattern from the fabric layers. Gently separate the fabric layers, pulling until the loops have been stretched as far as they will go. Cut each loop carefully between the fabric layers, leaving the threads to mark the points.*

Tracing Wheel

1 *Unpin the pattern where the marks are to be made, but leave it attached elsewhere. Slide a folded piece of contrasting dressmaker's carbon between the fabric layers on the wrong side as carbon marks are indelible.*

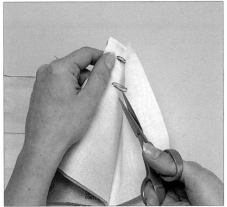

2 *Holding the tracing wheel firmly, run the teeth along the seamline, dart or other mark being transferred. This method is useful for marking darts and curved lines, but the wheel will make holes in the pattern, weakening it.*

Seam Gauge

This handy little tool is a miniature ruler with a central slide that can be set to the width of the seam allowance. Hold the flat edge of the slide against the raw cut edge of the fabric and use a pencil or other marker to mark the seamline.

Understanding Fabric

THERE ARE SO MANY DIFFERENT fabrics available today that it would be impossible to enumerate them all, but most fabrics share certain characteristics. Woven fabrics, such as the ones shown here, are by far the most numerous, but there are also nonwoven fabrics, mainly felt and interfacing, knits, and lace and net, which are composed of threads knotted into highly intricate patterns.

Warp and Weft

All woven fabrics have a warp (the threads that run lengthwise in the loom) and a weft (threads woven in and out of the warp threads at a right angle to create the widthwise grain). The weft is also called the woof. The selvedge is the tightly woven border that forms the lengthwise fabric edge. The lengthwise and widthwise grains are firm, without much give. However, when the fabric is folded or cut at a 45-degree angle to the selvedge, the fabric becomes easy to stretch. This grain is called the bias.

Velvet   **Plain-weave patterned cotton**   **Jacquard**

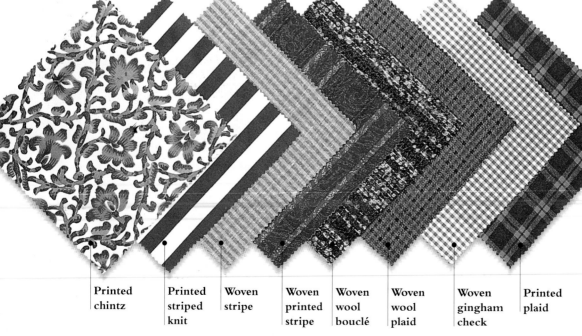

Printed chintz   **Printed striped knit**   **Woven stripe**   **Woven printed stripe**   **Woven wool bouclé**   **Woven wool plaid**   **Woven gingham check**   **Printed plaid**

Patterns

Patterns can be woven into the fabric, as is usually the case with plaids, checks and some stripes, or printed on the right-side surface after it is woven. Most chintzes and calico prints fall into this second group. Regular patterns must be matched in all sewing projects to achieve a professional-looking finish.

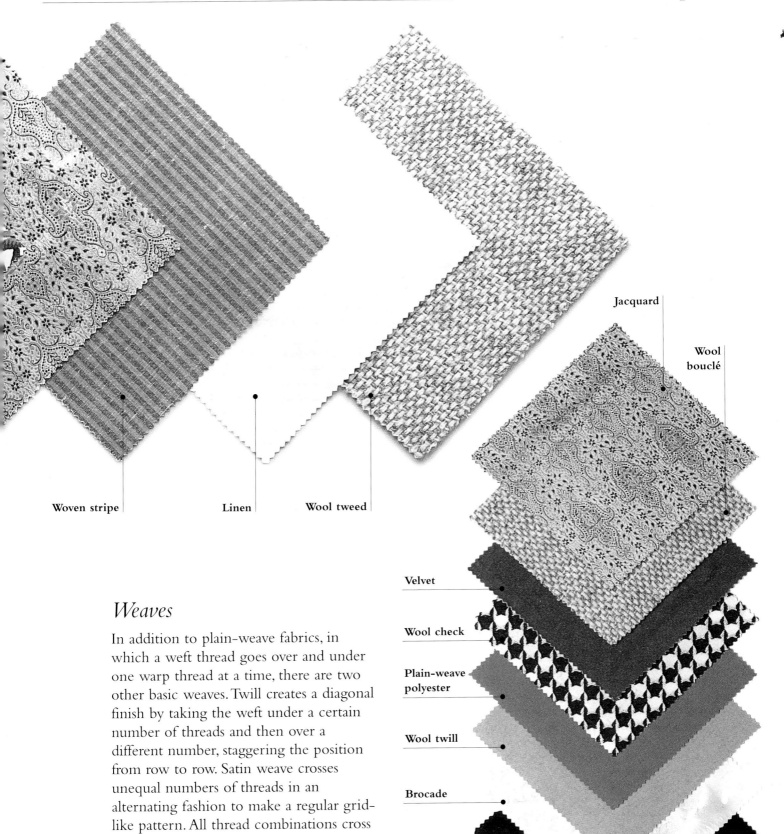

Woven stripe

Linen

Wool tweed

Jacquard

Wool bouclé

Velvet

Wool check

Plain-weave polyester

Wool twill

Brocade

Velvet

Cotton flannel

Terrycloth towelling

Weaves

In addition to plain-weave fabrics, in which a weft thread goes over and under one warp thread at a time, there are two other basic weaves. Twill creates a diagonal finish by taking the weft under a certain number of threads and then over a different number, staggering the position from row to row. Satin weave crosses unequal numbers of threads in an alternating fashion to make a regular grid-like pattern. All thread combinations cross each other at right angles.

Pile and nap weaves have a raised surface. Pile is a velvety surface created by weaving in extra threads that rise above the woven surface of the fabric. Nap is a woolly surface made by brushing up the fibers on the right side of the fabric.

Understanding Your Machine

EVERY SEWING MACHINE IS DIFFERENT and the best way to become familiar with yours is to use it. When buying a machine, consider the price, the immediate use you will put it to, what your long-term aspirations might be and whether you are able to handle its complexities. Always try out a machine before buying. If possible, see a demonstration by someone who knows the machine and its capabilities and take advantage of any classes offered by the sewing-machine manufacturers.

The Sewing Machine

All sewing machines have certain common features. The diagram below will help you understand the basic parts all machines share, but remember that the same knob or button may be in a different position on your machine. Some machines have a double thread spindle, for instance, and the sequence for threading, and the levers which carry the thread, will vary slightly in looks and positioning. The instruction manual will give specific information for your machine.

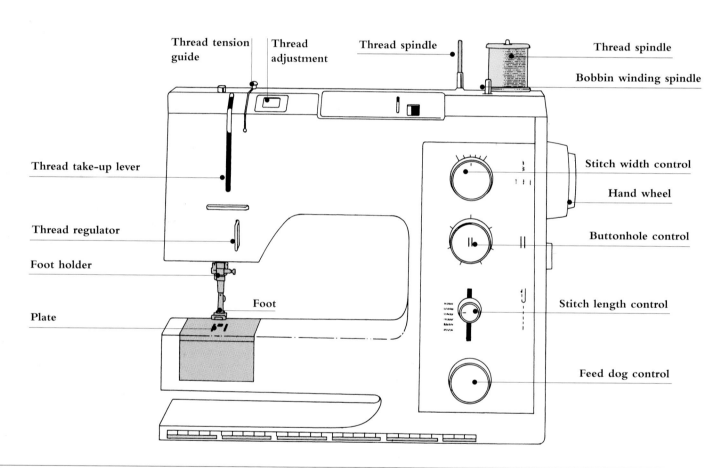

Thread tension guide · Thread adjustment · Thread spindle · Thread spindle · Bobbin winding spindle · Thread take-up lever · Stitch width control · Hand wheel · Thread regulator · Buttonhole control · Foot holder · Foot · Stitch length control · Plate · Feed dog control

Threading the Machine

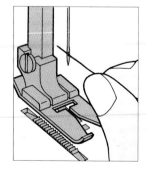

Threading the Needle
Always use a sharp needle that is appropriate to the fabric and make sure it is positioned properly. Check the instruction manual and insert the thread through the eye of the needle in the direction stated. Pull it through from the other side and allow enough length to give a smooth start to the stitching.

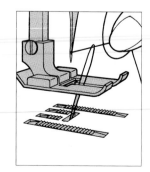

Pulling up the Bobbin Thread
Once the needle is threaded, put the bobbin in its case as shown in the manual, leaving a long end trailing below the machine plate. Turn the wheel once by hand. The top thread should catch the bobbin thread and pull it to the top as a loop. Use your fingers or a pin to pull the end through to the top.

Thread Tension

Thread tension must be balanced top and bottom to achieve a perfect stitch. Most new machines can adjust tension internally, but older models may need to be adjusted by hand – when switching from lightweight to heavyweight fabric, for example.

Balanced stitch

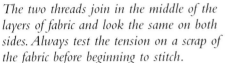

The two threads join in the middle of the layers of fabric and look the same on both sides. Always test the tension on a scrap of the fabric before beginning to stitch.

Bottom thread is too tight

If the bottom thread lies in a line and the top thread shows through onto the back of the seam, the bobbin thread tension is too tight. Loosen the bobbin thread according to the instructions in the manual; usually a screw in the bobbin case needs adjusting.

Top thread is too tight

If the top thread lies in a line and the bobbin thread is visible on top of the seam, the tension on the thread in the needle is too tight. Loosen the needle thread according to the instructions in the manual.

ACCESSORIES

Most new machines come with a basic package of accessories, from two or three extra feet to a small bottle of machine oil and a dusting brush. Check with the manufacturer for an up-to-date catalog of accessories for your particular machine so you can buy the more specialized parts as needed.

Shanks

Many of the feet available are interchangeable between machines and sometimes even between brands. Before buying a new foot, however, you need to know the style of shank for your machine. Check with the manual or the manufacturer to find out whether the machine has a low, high, super-high or slanted shank.

Low shank

High shank

Super-high shank

Slanted shank

Feet

By changing the feet you can create a range of special sewing effects. The choice of feet for new machines is often dauntingly extensive; many are very specialized and may not be of much use to you. There are, however, a number of types that are worth investing in if they do not come with the machine.

Darning/Quilting/Embroidery foot
All these feet have an open ring shape and are generally used with the feed dog down for free-machine embroidery, meander quilting and darning.

Buttonhole foot
There are numerous types of feet for making buttonholes. Some machines have a built-in buttonhole function, allowing buttonholes to be stitched with a standard presser foot.

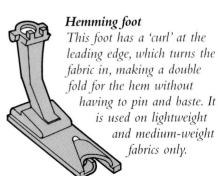
Zipper Foot
A zipper foot is essential for putting in a zipper neatly, and makes inserting piping into seams much easier. The needle can be used on each side in turn, so that the foot fits close to the zipper teeth.

Pintuck foot
Ridges on the underside of this foot allow the fabric to be drawn up into small tucks, stitched in even rows. The fabric needs little or no marking for tucks with this foot.

Hemming foot
This foot has a 'curl' at the leading edge, which turns the fabric in, making a double fold for the hem without having to pin and baste. It is used on lightweight and medium-weight fabrics only.

Stitches

SEWING IS ALL ABOUT STITCHES; in combination, stitches create seams to secure the pieces that make up sewn articles. Stitches can be decorative or invisible, and can be made by hand or worked by machine. Information on knotting, threading and fastening off, as well as how to execute and when to employ basic hand and machine stitches, is found here.

Using a Needle Threader

A needle threader consists of a loop of fine wire attached to a small metal plate. Hold the needle in your left hand and the threader plate in your right. Slip the wire through the eye, slide the end of the thread through the loop, and pull the loop back out of the eye, bringing the thread through the eye with it.

Knotting Thread

1 *A knot at the end of a length of thread is needed to hold it securely when stitching. Hold the needle between the right thumb and first finger with the point upward. Loop the end of the thread around the needle once or twice, holding it tightly in place.*

2 *Holding the loop of thread securely between thumb and finger, pull the loop down the entire length of thread to the end. The knot will catch when the end is reached.*

Quick Knotting

Hold the needle in the right hand so the thread cannot slip out. Loop the loose end of the thread around the first finger once or twice. Hold the loop securely between the thumb and finger, and roll it off the end of the finger into a knot.

Using a Thimble

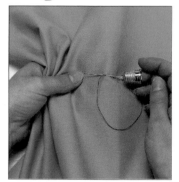

Some sewers always use a thimble; others never do. A thimble is especially useful if you are sewing heavyweight fabric. Place the thimble over the tip of the middle finger of the hand that is stitching and press the end of the needle with it gently.

Finishing Off

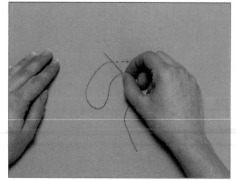

1 *At the end of a row of stitching, or when the thread is not long enough to work comfortably, take a small stitch on the wrong side of the fabric next to the last stitch made.*

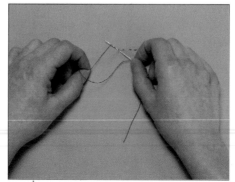

2 *Hold the needle steady in the right hand and wrap the thread two or three times around the point.*

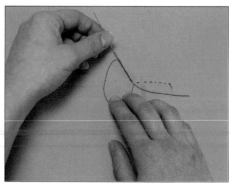

3 *Draw the needle through the wrapped loops and carefully pull the thread tight to form a secure knot.*

Basic Hand-Sewing Stitches

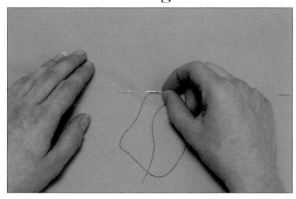

Basting

A basting stitch, also known as a tacking stitch, is a long stitch used to hold pieces of fabric in place until they have been sewn together permanently. Basting stitches are removed after the permanent stitching has been done. To baste, knot the end of a single or double length of contrasting-color thread and work a long running stitch through all the layers of fabric.

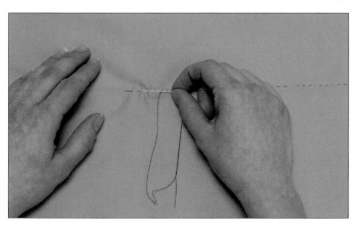

Backstitch

Backstitch is a strong stitch, ideal for seams and mending. Take the needle through all the layers of fabric, then insert it back a short distance behind where it first came out. Bring the point out ahead of the resulting stitch to the same length in front of the needle, and continue. Backstitches worked on top of each other at the beginning and end of the seams can be used for fastening off.

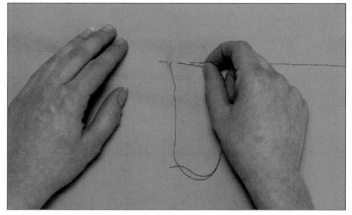

Running Stitch

A running stitch can be used to join seams that will not be subjected to strain, and for gathering fabric and making tucks by hand. Take the needle in and out of the fabric several times, picking up small, evenly spaced stitches. Pull the needle through the fabric until the thread is taut, and repeat to continue stitching.

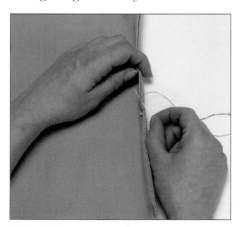

Slipstitch

This is invisible and used mainly to join folded edges of fabric together. Work with a single thread, knotted at one end. Hide the knot in the folded fabric edge and pull the thread out on one edge. Pick up one or two threads in the opposite edge and insert the needle back in the first side, next to where the thread came out. Slide the needle along inside of the fold a short distance and repeat to continue stitching.

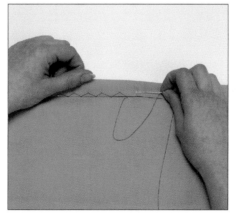

Herringbone Stitch

This stitch is useful for hemming and decoration. Working from left to right with the fabric flat, take a long diagonal stitch across the edge being secured, and take a backstitch into, but not through, the folded fabric of the hem. Bring the needle across in the opposite diagonal direction and pick up a few threads of fabric with a single backstitch. Repeat. One row of tiny stitches will be visible on the right side.

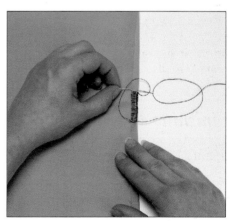

Buttonhole/Blanket Stitch

Buttonhole stitch makes a firm, strong edge finish and is used primarily for buttonholes. Blanket stitch is worked in the same way with the stitches farther apart. Insert the needle through the fabric from the raw edge, working with the needle pointing toward the fabric and away from the edge. Loop thread under the point of the needle, then pull through to create a ridge of thread along the edge.

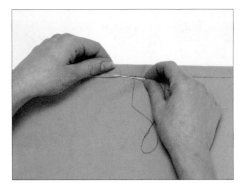

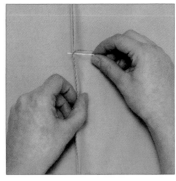

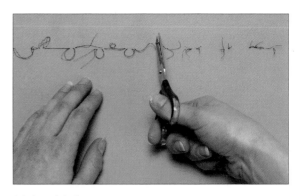

Hemming Stitch

A basic hemming stitch is used on most types of hems. Working from right to left, secure the thread inside the turned-under edge of the hem and bring it out. Pick up a few threads from the wrong side of the garment, then take a diagonal stitch through the turned-under edge. Pull through and repeat. For other hemming stitches, see page 65.

Overcasting

Overcasting, or oversewing, is used to finish raw edges, particularly on seams worked in fabrics that fray easily. Secure the thread with a few backstitches or a knot and work equally spaced diagonal stitches over the folded raw edges.

Tailor's Tacks

Tailor's tacks can mark two layers of fabric without drawn lines. They can be worked in a line or worked singly. Pin the pattern in place and use a double length of thread to stitch through all layers. Take another stitch in the same spot and make a generous loop. Repeat along the line. When all marks have been transferred, cut through the center of each long joining thread. Unpin pattern, separate fabric layers and stretch the loops to their limit. Cut each loop between layers, leaving the threads to mark points.

Hand-Sewn Thread Loop

Loops made from thread can be used as belt loops, especially on delicate fabrics, and with hook fasteners instead of the usual metal eyes or bars. They can also be used instead of buttonholes when worked on the edge of a buttonhole band.

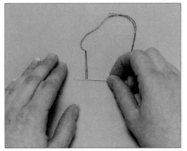

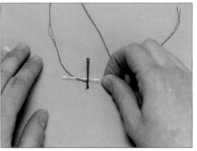

1 *First secure the thread in position at one end of the loop. Take two or three long stitches to the length of loop required, working them side by side on the right side of the fabric, and secure again.*

2 *Working over the long threads but not through the fabric, make a row of tightly spaced buttonhole stitches (see page 33) along the entire length, taking the thread under the needle point on each stitch. Ease each loop against the next.*

3 *The finished loop appears on the right side of the garment. Thicker thread loops can be made by sewing more long stitches initially.*

Hand-Sewn Bar Tack

Bar tacks are used to reinforce small areas that may be subjected to strain, such as the ends of hand-stitched buttonholes or seams. They are particularly useful for strengthening the ends of slits in necklines or hems.

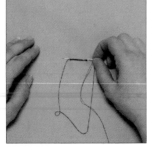

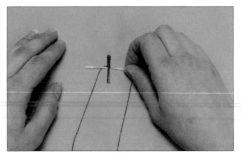

1 *To begin, work two or three stitches of equal length in the same spot at the point to be stitched.*

2 *Make a row of tightly spaced buttonhole stitches (see page 33) along the stitches, working over the combined threads and through the fabric. Loop the thread under the point of the needle on each stitch.*

3 *The finished bar tack can be made to any length that is appropriate.*

Hand-Sewn Arrowhead Tack

Arrowhead tacks are triangular decorative stitches, generally used in the right side of the garment to strengthen and reinforce weak points.

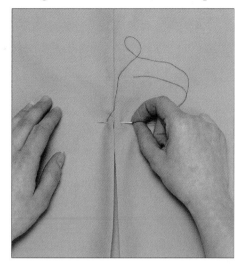

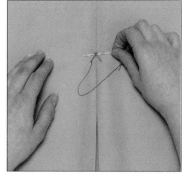

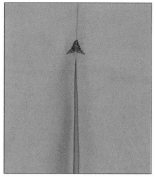

1 Insert needle from the wrong side so the thread is on the left side of the bottom of the point being reinforced. Take a tiny stitch at the arrowhead top from right to left. Bring the needle down to the right side of the bottom point and insert at the same level as the beginning stitch.

2 Bring the needle out next to the starting point, to the inside of the triangle. Take a stitch at the top, just below the previous stitch. Repeat, working toward bottom center of the arrowhead in each direction, and bringing the top stitches down until the threads meet in the center.

3 The finished arrowhead gives a neat attractive strength to the top of a kick pleat, and adds a decorative touch. The stitch is equally successful on other pleats and at the ends of pockets, and can be worked using stranded embroidery thread.

Basic Machine Stitches

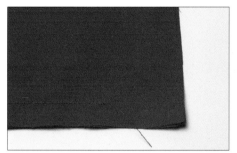

Straight Stitch

A straight line of machine stitching is the simplest stitch used to join fabric pieces. Run several practice seams on different fabrics and become familiar with the machine before working on a garment. Follow the marked seamline, or the width guidelines marked on the machine plate.

Backstitch

Backstitch the ends of seams to secure them. Insert the needle 1/2 in (1.25 cm) from the beginning edge and use the reverse setting on the machine to stitch back to the beginning. Stitch the seam. At the end of the seam, use the reverse setting to stitch back over the final few stitches.

Machine Basting

Machine basting is used to join pieces of fabric temporarily so they can be tried on and adjusted before final stitching. Loosen the tension, set the longest stitch length and stitch a seam. Do not backstitch the ends. To remove, clip top thread every few stitches and pull out the bobbin thread.

Staystitching

Staystitching is a row of straight stitch on edges liable to stretch, such as curved necklines or shoulder a point. Staystitching should be worked just inside the marked seam-line, before any other handling of the fabric. Edge stitching is a row of straight stitch worked along the raw edge.

Zigzag Stitch

Most modern machines have a zigzag setting. Zigzag stitch can finish raw edges to prevent them from fraying, and zigzag seams are the best way to join stretch fabrics. Tight zigzag makes a firm satin stitch. Set zigzag function to the desired width and length and stitch as usual.

Gathering Stitch

This gives more evenly spaced gathers than hand-gathering. Use longest stitch and work just inside the seamline. Run another row of long stitching just outside seamline. Pull bobbin threads of both rows to gather. Baste and stitch seam between rows, then remove gathering threads.

Seams

SEAMS ARE ROWS OF STITCHES used to hold pieces of fabric together. Although they are usually stitched by machine, they can be made by hand. Backstitch is the best stitch to use for hand-sewn seams. The type of seam, as well as the way in which its raw edges are finished, depends on the fabric and design of the item being stitched. Between the stitched seamline and the raw edge is the seam allowance, which is usually ⅝ in (16 mm) on commercial patterns.

Flat Seam

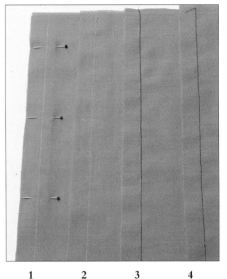

1 ◄► 2 ◄► 3 ◄► 4 ►

A plain basic seam, worked in a machine straight stitch, is the type used for most sewing, from dressmaking and home sewing to patchwork. First mark the seamline on the wrong side of the fabric and pin the pieces together with right sides facing (1). Baste along the marked seamline and remove the pins (2). Work a row of straight stitch along basted seamline (3). Remove the basting threads (4). Finally, press the finished seam as instructed, either open or to one side.

Double Seam

A double seam combines the seam stitching and the seam finishing, making a narrow double seam that is particularly useful on sheer or lightweight fabric. The inside seam can also be zigzagged, which is ideal for knitted jerseys. To make a double seam, stitch along the marked seamline, then stitch in the seam allowance, about ⅛ in (3 mm) away from the seamline. Trim away excess fabric along the raw edge, close to the stitching, and press seam to one side.

Turning a Corner

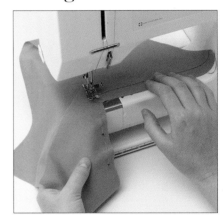

To turn a corner in a seam in any direction, keep the needle in the fabric when the corner is reached. Lift the presser foot and swivel the fabric so that the new side of the corner is lined up as shown. Continue stitching as usual.

Intersecting Seams

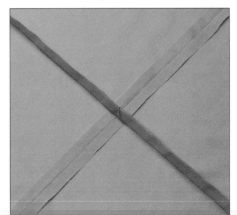

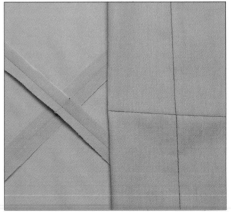

1 *To join two seams at precise right angles, make flat seams in the pieces to be joined and press open. Mark the joining seamline on one piece only. With right sides together, match the stitched seams precisely and place a pin through both stitched seams at the joining point.*

2 *Pin along the length of the joining seam and baste if necessary. Stitch a flat seam along the marked seamline. To reduce bulk from the intersection, cut the seam allowance away to make a point on both sides of the seam, as shown.*

3 *Press the new seam open, as shown left. The finished seam should form a precise four-cornered right angle at the meeting point, as shown right.*

French Seam

A French seam is a very narrow seam that is used mainly on delicate fabrics and those that fray easily.

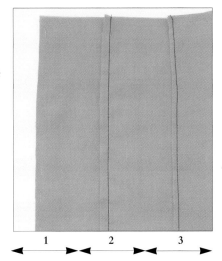

1 With wrong sides together, pin and baste along the seamline (1). Stitch a flat seam just inside the seamline, pressing it flat as you work (2). Trim the seam allowance to 1/8 in (3 mm) (3). Press the seam open.

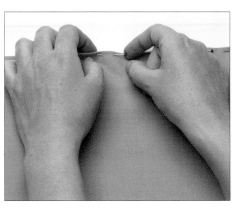

2 Turn the fabric right sides together along the stitched seamline and press. Pin, then baste the seam through the two layers of fabric only, so that the raw edges are enclosed between the seams.

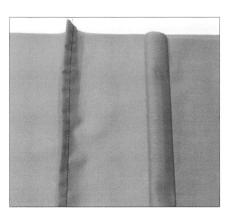

3 Stitch along the basted seamline and press to one side. The finished seam encloses the raw edges completely on the wrong side, as shown left, and looks like a flat seam from the right side of the garment, as shown right.

Flat Fell Seam

Like the French seam, this seam encloses the raw edges, but it also incorporates a line of decorative stitching. It is widely used in making clothes that will be subjected to heavy wear, such as sports clothes.

1 With wrong sides together, pin and baste along the seamline; then stitch a flat seam. Press the seam open, then press it again to one side. Trim away the seam allowance on one side, the under layer, to half its width.

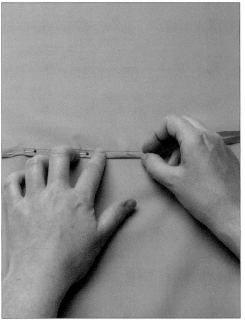

2 Open the piece out flat and fold the wider seam allowance, the upper layer, over to enclose the trimmed layer. Pin in place along the fold. Stitch along the edge of the fold, removing pins as you work.

3 The finished seam is double-stitched on the right side of the garment, as shown here on the left. On the wrong side, shown here on the right, the seam appears as a flat seam with a single row of stitching alongside it.

Topstitched Seam

Topstitching consists of a row of straight machine stitching (see page 35) along the outside of a finished edge. A topstitched seam, single or double, finishes the raw edges of seams to prevent fraying and gives a decorative effect.

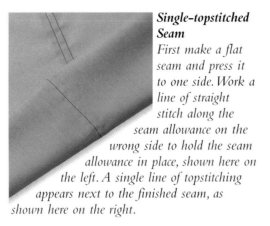

Single-topstitched Seam
First make a flat seam and press it to one side. Work a line of straight stitch along the seam allowance on the wrong side to hold the seam allowance in place, shown here on the left. A single line of topstitching appears next to the finished seam, as shown here on the right.

Double-topstitched Seam
Make a flat seam and press it open. Work a line of straight stitch down one side of the seam allowance, then repeat along the other side, equidistant from the seam. The flat seam will lie in the center of the rows of topstitching and needs no further finishing. The finished seam is shown from the wrong side (left) and from the right side (right).

Seam Finishes

Finishing seams by stitching or securing the raw edges of the seam allowance will give the seam a more professional appearance and will help prevent fraying and general wear and tear.

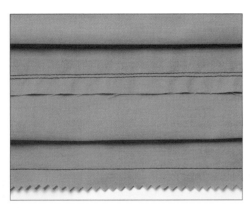

Simple Finishes
Top: *The seam is pressed open and the raw edges are zigzagged separately, worked as close to the edge as possible. This finish is suitable for all weights of fabrics that have a tendency to fray.*
Center: *The seam is pressed to one side and a second row of stitching is made in the seam allowance, close to the seamline. This method is particularly useful for strengthening seams that are subject to strain.*
Bottom: *The seam is pressed to one side and the doubled raw edge trimmed with pinking shears. This is a quick method that is good for most seams.*

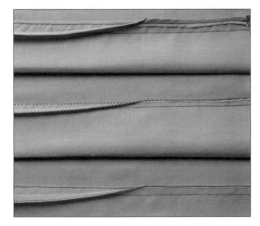

Tailored Finishes
Top: *Pin a length of narrow bias binding over each raw edge to enclose, then stitch through all layers close to the edge of the binding. Suitable for any seam, particularly for those seams that fray easily.*
Center: *Turn under a single hem along each raw edge. Zigzag along each folded edge. Particularly suitable for lightweight fabrics and those that fray easily.*
Bottom: *Turn under, pin and stitch a single hem along each raw edge of the seam. As this finish creates extra bulk, it is not suitable for heavy fabrics.*

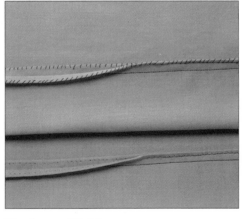

Hand-sewn Finishes
Top: *A row of evenly spaced overcasting is stitched along each raw edge. This finish is especially suitable for heavyweight fabrics.*
Bottom: *Turn under a double hem along each raw edge and a work a row of hand-hemming. Like its machine counterpart, a hand-hemmed finish is good for lightweight and delicate fabrics, but unsuitable for heavyweight ones.*

SEAMS ON JERSEY

Knitted fabrics need slightly different seam treatments than plain-weave fabrics. Always stitch with a ballpoint needle. Left: The simple seam is zigzagged with a short length and narrow stitch width. The zigzagging eases the tension but looks like an ordinary flat seam. Center: A special overlock setting, available on many machines, is stitched along the edge of the seam. It is good for seams that will not be subjected to strain. Right: The seam on the right combines the first two to give a strong seam that is unlikely to fray and will withstand strain.

Clipping Corners

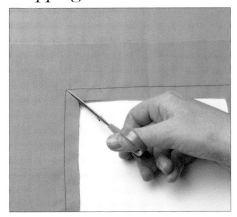
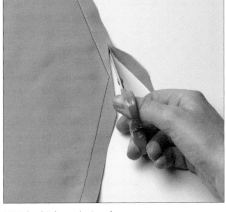

Right Angle
Holding a pair of small sharp scissors at a 45-degree angle to the corner, clip into the seam allowance, up to but not through the stitching.

Wide (Obtuse) Angle
Use sharp dressmaking scissors to cut off the point of the angle in one snip, as close to the stitching as possible without cutting through the seam.

Sharp (Acute) Angle
Use small sharp scissors to cut into the center of the stitched point, up to but not through the seam.

Clipping Curves

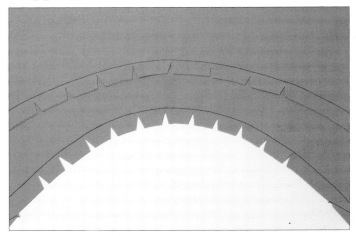
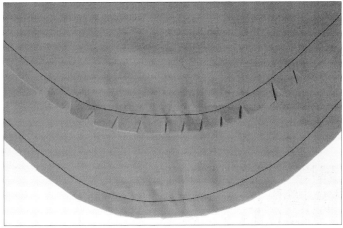

Concave Curves
The tension in the curve on concave seams must be eased, so clip the seam with small, sharp scissors at right angles to the stitching. Cut up to, but not through, the seam. When the seam is turned right side out, the clipping allows the seam to be pressed flat. The technique is the same if the curve is shallow or deep, as shown above.

Convex Curves
Convex curves need to have fabric removed to reduce the bulk in the seam allowance. Using small sharp scissors, cut a series of notches up to but not through the stitching. The fabric will lie flat when turned right side out.

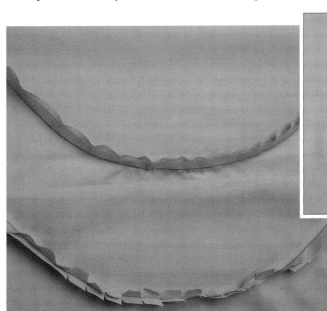

Combination Curves
To ease the tension on a seam joining a concave curve to a convex one, clip at a right angle into the seam allowance, as for convex curves. Press the seam toward the convex side to make the piece lie flat. The unclipped seam is shown on the far left and the clipped and pressed seam is shown on the right. Inset: From the right side, the seam looks neat and the garment will take the extra strain of the curves.

Pressing and Mitering

NO MATTER HOW ACCURATELY stitched the seams or how fine the hems, pressing as you work is the key to professional-looking results. (Markings, such as tucks and pleats, can be pressed first, before stitching.) You can use either a dry iron or steam, depending on the fabric.

Pressing is different from ironing. It is done lightly, with the tip of the iron, on specific areas. Never press over zippers, pockets or thick seams, which can all leave marks on the right side of the fabric.

Accurate pressing is also crucial to mitering, which is a useful way of finishing a corner neatly with a 45-degree angle for hemming right-angled corners.

PRESSING CHART	
HEAT	**FABRIC**
Low	Acetate, Shiny Surfaces
Low to Moderate	Blends, Nylon, Pile/Nap, Polyester, Rayon, Silk
Moderate	Acylic, Blends, Wool
Moderate to High	Cotton
High	Linen

USEFUL TIPS

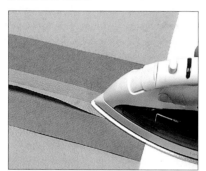

Pressing with Paper
To press seams open without leaving a mark on the right side, cut strips of brown paper and slide a strip under the seam allowance on each side before pressing. Paper strips can also be used to press pleats on fabrics that might be marked by pressing.

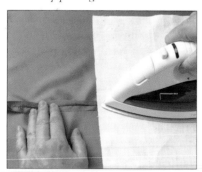

Press Cloth
A press cloth can be used to prevent the shininess that occurs on many fabrics when they are pressed. The ideal cloth to use is a piece of clean cotton or linen sheeting. Place the cloth on the fabric and press as usual. If you use a dry iron, dampen the cloth to provide extra moisture.

Pressing

Flat seam
Remove all pins and basting threads; they are likely to leave marks on the fabric. Using the tip of the iron on the wrong side of the sewn piece, open the seam and slide the iron gently but firmly along the length of the seam.

Hems
All hems should be pressed from the fold toward the stitched edge. Steam pressing will help shrink fullness, especially in a curved hem. Leave the basting in place and press with the tip of the iron into the fabric. Remove the basting and press again to remove marks left by the threads.

Clipped seam
Where a seam has been clipped, lay the piece flat on the ironing board and use the point of the iron to press each section open by pressing the top layer of the seam back onto the fabric.

Fingerpressing
It is possible to press seams open on firmly woven or pile fabrics simply by placing the piece on a hard flat surface and running a fingertip down the length of the seam, from top to bottom. Widely used in patchwork, fingerpressing is not suitable for knitted fabrics or those that fray easily.

Mitered Hem

1 *At the corner to be mitered, turn the seam allowances to the right side and press along the seamlines. Open flat again and turn back the triangle of corner fabric, aligning the pressed marks as shown; press along the diagonal fold.*

2 *Open the corner again and fold it diagonally, right sides together, so that the raw edges and the creases meet. Pin and stitch along the pressed diagonal line.*

3 *Trim the triangular piece of seam allowance from the corner, then press the seam open. Repeat for all the corners.*

4 *Turn the corners right side out to the wrong side of the fabric. Turn under the raw edges on each side of the hem and pin in place. Baste, then stitch in place to hem.*

5 *The finished miter makes a neat corner on the right side, here shown top. The corner seam appears on the wrong side, here shown bottom, but this side can be used decoratively, if desired.*

Mitering Binding

1 *This technique can be used to miter straight or bias binding. First stitch a separate strip of binding to each side of the piece with right sides together (see page 45), working only up to the point where the seamlines intersect at the corner. Fold up the excess binding at one corner, pinning in place. Mark the diagonal corner on both strips of binding, as shown. Repeat to mark other corners.*

2 *Pin and stitch the corner diagonal seam on the binding, starting at the point where the side seamlines meet and working out to the raw edge. Trim the seam allowance to reduce bulk. Repeat to stitch each corner seam.*

3 *Turn the corners right side out to the wrong side of the fabric. Turn under the binding along the foldline to conceal the raw edges. Pin, baste and stitch the binding in place, as in step 4 of the Mitered Hem above. The finished corner, shown here from the wrong side, is neat and sharp.*

MITERED TRIMS

Trims can be applied to edges and mitered at the corners. The lace trim, shown top, has first been sewn onto the right side of the fabric, with the mitered corner, then worked into the wrong side. The ribbon trim, shown bottom, is sewn as described in steps 1 and 2 of the Mitered Binding, then finished with top-stitching on the right side.

Gathers and Pleats

GATHERING AND PLEATING are both techniques for incorporating fullness in a seam. They are used in garments, particularly in skirts and sleeves, and on home furnishings from sofa covers to tablecloth edgings. Gathering consists of running a long thread by hand or machine down a length of fabric and pulling the thread up. Shirring is similar, with rows of cord or elastic instead of threads to create a smocked effect. Pleats are folds in the fabric, anchored at the top and allowed to fall neatly to the bottom. Lightweight fabrics can be folded lengthwise to make a double ruffle and will drape softly when gathered or pleated; heavier weights of fabric will create stiffer folds.

Gathering

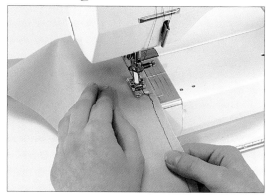

1 *Measure, mark and cut the fabric to be gathered, as necessary. Set the sewing machine on the longest stitch length and run a double row of gathering stitch along the edge to be gathered. Make the first row inside the seam allowance, then work the second row just outside the seamline. Leave the threads long at both ends.*

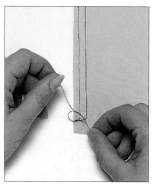

2 *Separate each loose long thread from the others at one end. Tie the two top threads together, and then repeat with the bottom bobbin threads.*

3 *Holding the ruffle along the stitched edge, pull the bobbin thread of each row at the untied end gently along the entire length of the fabric. Adjust the gathers evenly as you work until the fabric is gathered up to the required length. Knot the thread ends to secure the gathers.*

4 *Adjust the machine to a normal setting. Finish by assembling the pattern pieces. Most often this will require pinning and stitching the gathered fabric to an ungathered piece along the raw edges. Stitch the seam between the rows of gathering stitch so that the seam allowance on the gathered piece will be even. Remove all gathering and basting threads from the finished piece.*

Shirring

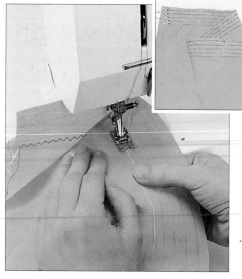

1 *Mark the lines to be shirred on the fabric. Cut lengths of fine cord, about 6 in (15 cm) longer than the width of the fabric. Set the sewing machine to a wide zigzag stitch. Place one cord along each marked line and stitch over the cord to secure it to the fabric, backstitching at both ends. Make sure the cord is not caught in the stitching. Leave a length of cord free at each end of every row. Inset: Knot each cord separately on one end of the piece.*

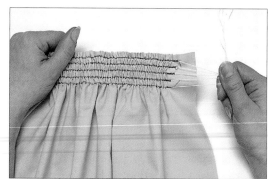

2 *Holding the fabric firmly at the knotted end, pull gently on the loose cords at the opposite end. Pull up until the piece is gathered up to the desired length. Knot the ends of the cords to secure the shirring. Finish by assembling the piece as required.*

Knife Pleats

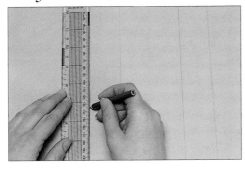

1 Knife pleats are all folded in the same direction. Using a ruler and fabric marker, draw lines on the wrong side of the fabric to mark the foldlines and placement lines and, if necessary, the bottom of the pleats. If desired, use a different-color marker for the fold lines and the placement lines.

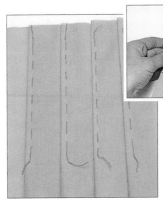

2 Using the pattern piece as a guide, fold the pleats along the marked lines. Pin and baste each pleat in place on the right side, from top to bottom. Pin along the top of the pleats, well inside the seam allowance. Inset: Baste, then stitch to secure the pleats in place.

3 Topstitch along the top folded edge of each pleat from the top to the bottom marked line. The stitching shown here is for deep pleats, but stitching can be short, just enough to hold the pleat in place at the top. For sharp pleats, press before removing the basting stitches; for soft pleats, remove the basting and then press. Sharp pleats that go to the hem should be hemmed before being pressed.

Inverted Box Pleats

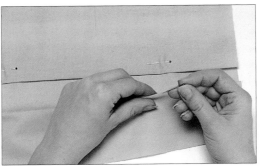

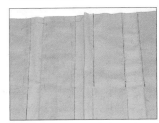

1 In inverted pleats, the foldlines are on the right side of the fabric; on box pleats, the foldlines are behind the center piece (see Other Box Pleats, right). Mark the foldlines and bottom guidelines on right side of the fabric, as in step 1 of Knife Pleats, above.

2 Fold each pleat into the center to meet the one opposite. Pin in place. The pleats shown here are stitched together along the foldline; pin pleats along the foldlines with right sides together before stitching. Remove pins as you work.

3 Stitch along the foldlines to the bottom of the marked pleat, backstitching at each end to secure.

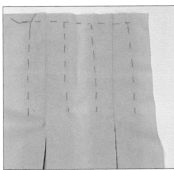

4 Press the pleats flat with the stitched foldlines in the center of the underpleats. Baste along the top edge and the folded edges of each underpleat.

5 To finish, stitch a double-topstitched seam (see page 38) along the edge of the center seam to the bottom of each pleat if desired. Then remove the basting and press again.

OTHER BOX PLEATS

Box pleats are made in exactly the same way as inverted box pleats, but the center pleat is on the right side of the garment with the folded edges meeting behind it. The example shown here has been topstitched along the folded edges of the center pleat.

Bindings and Borders

RAW EDGES ON GARMENTS and home furnishings must be finished to prevent them from fraying, and often the finishing can be decorative. Although hems (see page 64) are the most usual way of finishing, binding with bias or straight strips of fabric is another useful method. Trims and borders, such as piping and ruffles, are also simple and effective finishes for edges and seams.

Making a Bias Binding

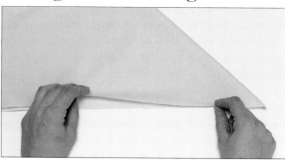

1 *Making a strip of bias binding means fabrics can be matched exactly in a sewing project, which is not possible with ready-made binding. First level the edges of the fabric along the straight grain in both directions. Fold the corner so that the straight edges match; the fold lies along the bias.*

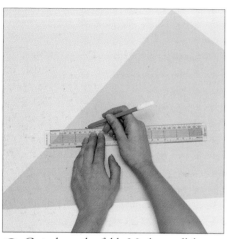

2 *Cut along the fold. Mark parallel lines along the bias to the required width of the binding. Using a water-soluble marker, number the rows as shown, staggering the numbers so the first row on the left-hand side is 1, the first row on the right-hand side is 2, the second row on the left-hand side is 2, and so on.*

3 *Fold the piece with right sides together. Stitch to join the numbered edges, matching the numbers – 2 to 2, 3 to 3, 4 to 4, and so on – to make a tube. The strip numbered 1 and the final strip on the opposite side will not be stitched.*

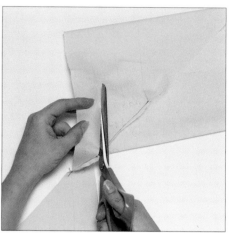

4 *Press the seam open. Cut along the marked line on the tube, which is now a continuous spiral running from one end of the tube to the other.*

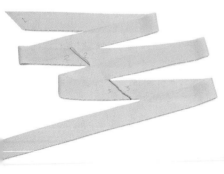

5 *The finished bias binding strip is numbered in order at each seam. Remove all of the markings and then press the seams again.*

6 *To finish, fold both long edges to the center and press them in place. Work carefully to prevent stretching. Fold and press the strip lengthwise along the center. The strip is now ready to use.*

JOINING STRIPS

1 *To make a single long bias strip from two or more shorter strips, place two of the short edges together along the straight grain and pin together as shown.*

2 *Stitch the seam and press it open. Carefully trim away the pointed ends of the seam. Repeat to add more strips until you have reached the required length.*

Binding a Straight Edge

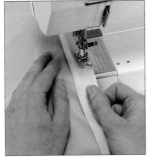
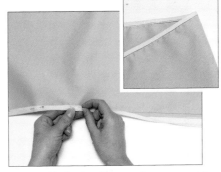

1 With right sides together and folds open, pin one edge of the bias binding to the raw edge of the fabric. Be careful not to stretch the binding out of shape.

2 Stitch along the foldline, removing the pins as you work. Press the seam carefully toward the binding.

3 Fold the binding to the wrong side. Pin in place with the folded edge turned under. Stitch along the edge by machine or hand. Inset: The stitching on the right side of the finished bound edge will be virtually invisible, hidden by the folded edge of the binding.

Binding and Mitering a Corner

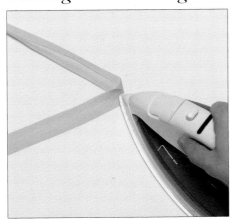
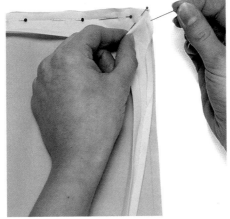
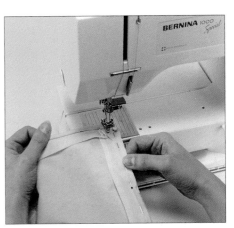

1 Mark the corner position on the binding by pressing. With the long edges pressed under, fold the bias binding along the straight grain and press. Fold and press again along the opposite straight grain. The two press marks cross in the center of the strip.

2 With right sides together, pin the center of the crossed mark to the corner point on the fabric being bound. Following the foldline, pin the binding in place along the two edges of the fabric. Repeat for all corners.

3 Stitch along the foldline to the corner, removing pins as you work. With the needle down in the corner point, lift the presser foot and turn the work (see page 36). Continue stitching along the foldline on the next side. Make sure the folded corner does not get caught in the stitching.

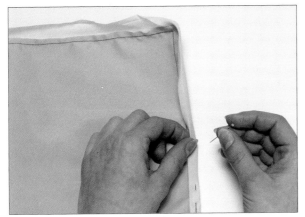
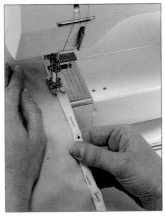

4 Fold the binding over to the wrong side and pin in place along the folded edge, as in step 3 of Binding a Straight Edge, above. Make sure the corners in the bias binding are neatly folded and pinned in place.

5 Stitch the binding along the folded edge on the wrong side of the work, as in step 3.

6 The finished corner is neatly folded at a 45-degree angle. This method works best with narrow bias binding.

PIPING

Piping is an attractive way to finish edges. It consists of a bias strip that is folded and inserted inside a seam, and the strip can be either plain or corded. Plain and corded piping can be used to trim and accent details anywhere on a garment, but they are always caught in the seam. Both are also useful ways of finishing the edges of cushions and other home furnishings.

Simple Piping

Cut a strip of bias binding to the length desired (see page 44) and twice the required width plus 1 in (2.5 cm). Fold lengthwise with wrong sides together and press lightly. Be careful not to stretch the strip. Stitch about ½ in (1.25 cm) from the raw edge, making sure the desired width of the piping is created.

Corded Piping

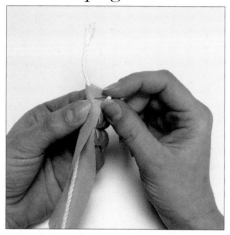

1 To make corded piping, prepare a strip of bias binding as for the simple piping above, folding lengthwise with wrong sides together. Lay the cord inside the binding and pin through the fabric and cord at one end to secure.

2 Using the zipper foot attachment on the sewing machine, stitch along the edge of, but not through, the cord. Keep the raw edges even and work the stitching with the foot as close as possible against the cord.

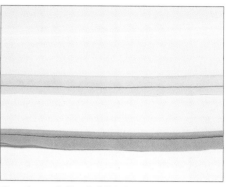

Simple and Corded Piping
Simple piping, shown top, is flat and works especially well with heavier weights of fabric that do not need a cord insert. Corded piping, shown bottom, has a ridged edge that is particularly useful for trimming cushions. The cord gives the piping extra strength and makes it easier to keep the piping even.

Applying Piping

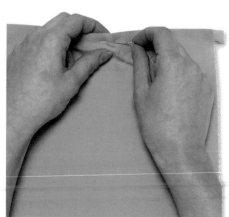

1 With right sides facing and raw edges aligned, pin and baste the fabric pieces together along the seamline, enclosing the plain or corded piping. Alternatively, baste the piping to one piece first before pinning and basting the second piece in place.

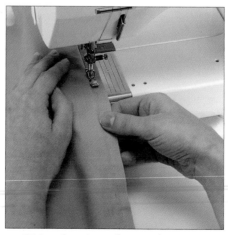

2 Using the zipper foot on the sewing machine for corded piping, and the presser foot for simple piping, stitch along the basted line.

Simple and Corded Piped Seams
The simple piping, shown top, has a softer look in the seam than the corded piping, shown bottom, which creates a strong, more sculptured, edge.

RUFFLES

Ruffles, also called frills, are gathered strips of matching or coordinated fabric applied to the edges of garments and home furnishings. They give a soft, feminine border to many types of sewn articles for the home, such as bedspreads and cushion covers. Many garments, from nightgowns to ballgowns, can be enhanced by judiciously positioned ruffles.

Simple Ruffle

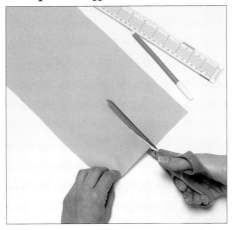

1 *Cut a strip of fabric to the desired width of the ruffle, plus hem and seam allowances. The strip should measure 2 to 3 times the desired finished length. Join strips along the short edges if necessary to make up the length.*

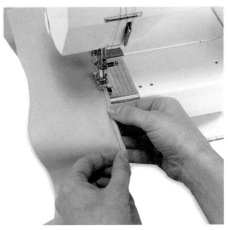

2 *Next turn under and stitch a narrow double hem along one long edge (see page 66), pinning and basting as necessary. Alternatively, you can use a hemming foot attachment on the sewing machine (see page 31).*

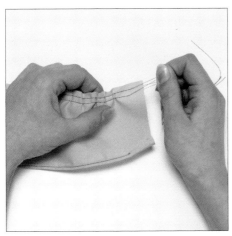

3 *Run a double row of gathering stitches along the long raw edge, 1/2 in (0.5 cm) apart, then pull up the gathers gently (see pages 35 and 42).*

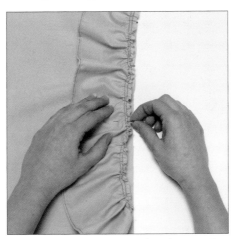

4 *When the ruffle is gathered up to the required length, pin it to the raw edge of the fabric with right sides together. Stitch in place.*

5 *When the ruffle has been stitched in place, press the seam toward the garment and carefully remove all the gathering stitches.*

APPLYING A RUFFLE TO A CUSHION

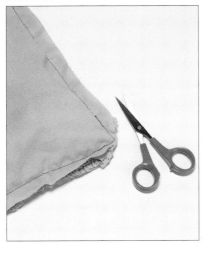

1 *With right sides together and raw edges aligned, pin and baste the ruffle to the front cushion piece, folding the ruffle around the corners. Pin the back cushion piece to the front, right sides together, enclosing the ruffle. Stitch the seam, leaving a 4-in (10-cm) gap for turning. Clip corners.*

2 *Turn the cover right side out through the gap. Insert the cushion pad, slipstitch the gap closed and press. The ruffle gives the finished cushion cover a soft edge. This technique can be used to attach all types of borders and trims to cushions, pillowcases and similar projects.*

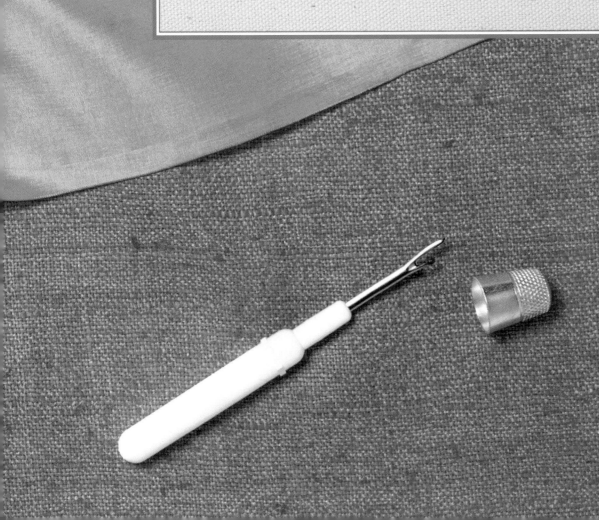

DRESSMAKING

All garments have common elements and this chapter breaks a typical garment into its component parts to show how to construct any garment you wish to make. Starting with elements of internal construction like darts and facings, the chapter moves step by step to sleeves, collars, waistbands, hems, pockets, fastenings and linings, and finishes with altering patterns and remodelling existing clothes.

Darts and Tucks

DARTS PROVIDE SHAPE AND STRUCTURE to many patterns, and they appear mostly at the bust, waist, shoulder and elbow. They are pointed folds that are stitched into the fabric and then pressed in specific ways. Generally, vertical darts are pressed downward and horizontal ones are pressed toward the center of the garment. Tucks, which are straight folds in the fabric, are similar to darts and add a decorative element and shape to a garment.

Darts

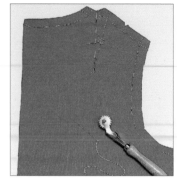

1 Darts are marked on the relevant pattern piece. Following the pattern guidelines carefully, mark and tack all stitching lines.

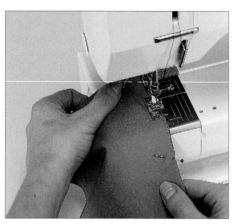

2 Stitch the dart toward the point. Finish a few stitches past the point, leaving approximately 4 in (10 cm) of thread free at the point.

3 Press the stitched dart on the wrong, and then the right, side of the garment so that it lies flat to one side. To fasten off, tie the threads left free in step 2 and snip the ends.

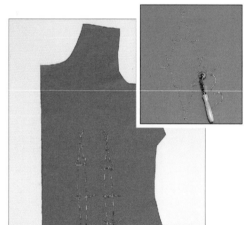

4 Double-pointed darts are prepared in the same way, beginning at the top point and stitching downward to finish at the bottom point. Inset: Press the stitched dart along its fold.

USEFUL TIP

Darts in heavyweight or loosely woven fabrics can be double-stitched to make them more secure. To fasten off, tie the thread ends at the point of the dart separately for each stitching line.

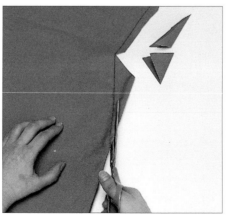

5 Double-pointed darts usually need to be cut. Cut away a triangle of fabric in the widest part of the dart, as shown. Do not cut into the stitching. Trim the folded edge of the dart ½ in (1.25 cm) from the stitched line in each direction, leaving the point uncut.

6 Carefully press half of the dart open and flat. Repeat for the other half of the dart.

Tucks

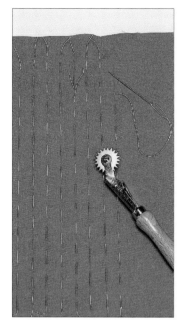

1 Tucks can be vertical, horizontal or even diagonal. To sew tucks, begin by transferring guidelines for the tucks to the wrong side of the fabric with a tracing wheel and dressmaker's tracing paper. Baste along each marked line.

• • • • • • • • • • • •

TECHNIQUES   **page**
Basting   **33**
Marking   **27**
Understanding patterns   **24**

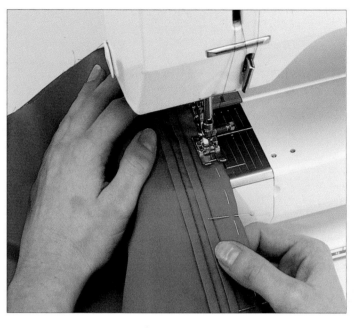

2 Make one tuck at a time. To do this, match two adjoining guidelines and pin the tuck in place, then stitch along the guideline. Repeat for each tuck. Remove the basting and press. Alternatively, you can use the edge of the presser foot or one of the guidelines marked on the footplate to guide the stitching.

USEFUL TIP

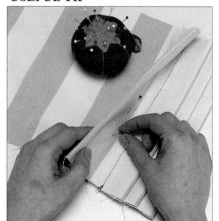

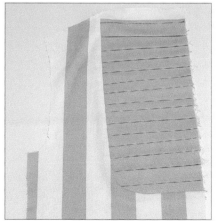

1 Working on striped or checked fabric can create very interesting effects. Here the tucks are the same width as the stripes on the fabric, and they are folded to leave a narrow band of the contrasting color along each fold.

2 This yoke, which was tucked before the pattern piece was cut out, appears as plain green. The tucks in the fabric are set horizontally to contrast effectively with the bold vertical stripes.

Have measuring and marking equipment on hand

Facings

A FACING IS A PIECE of fabric that provides a neat finish and added strength to external edges of a garment. Facings can be separate pieces stitched to the garment and then folded back, or cut as part of the garment piece. Most facings are made of the garment fabric, but they can be cut from lightweight fabric to reduce bulk. Interfacing, a thin layer of fabric that can be sewn or ironed on, is often used to strengthen facings further. It is available in a variety of weights and colors (see page 19).

Neckline
Facings enclose the raw edges of garments, particularly at points such as the neckline.

One-piece Facing

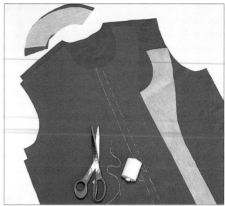

1 *Cut out pieces from fabric and iron-on interfacing. Prepare pieces to be faced by marking and basting.*

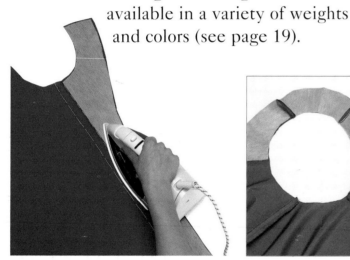

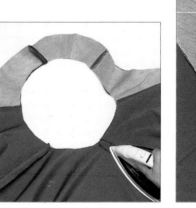

2 *Following the manufacturer's instructions, iron the interfacing in position on all the pieces.*

3 *Pin and stitch the interfaced pieces together along the marked seamlines. Press all seams open.*

4 *Turn back the straight edges along the foldline, as marked. Pin and baste the curved neckline seam in place. Stitch the seam and remove the basting.*

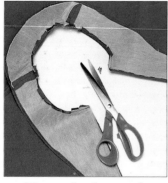

5 *Turn under the raw edge of the interfaced pieces and staystitch (see Useful Tips, right). Carefully trim the corners and clip the curved neckline seam at regular intervals.*

6 *Turn the interfaced pieces to the inside and press. Topstitch the edges, if desired.*

USEFUL TIPS

To ease curves, clip $^3/16$ in (3 mm) into the seam allowance before staystitching the edge (see right).

On either delicate or heavyweight fabrics, herringbone-stitch along the staystitched edge to secure it and prevent the edges from fraying (see below).

Herringbone Stitch

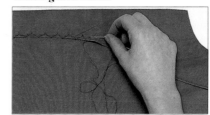

Clipped Curves

SEPARATE PIECES

1 *When making a two-piece facing (shown here in a contrasting color for clarity), cut out and prepare the pieces, applying interfacing if necessary.*

2 *Join the straight seams to attach the facing to the garment, then proceed as described in steps 3–6 of One-piece Facing.*

V-Neckline Facing

1 *Cut out pieces and a bias facing strip. Prepare the fabric piece by marking and basting the neck seamline. Staystitch a 'V', about ¾ in (2 cm) long, on the point of the seamline.*

2 *Stitch the shoulder seams, then baste the bias-cut neckband to the neck, leaving the final 2 in (5 cm) unsewn. Ease the back section between the shoulder seams so that the neckband lies flat.*

3 *Stitch the neckline seam, leaving the loose end unstitched. Working from the wrong side of the garment at the stitched end of the neckband, turn under a doubled hem and baste for 3 in (7.5 cm).*

4 *Match the unstitched edge of the neckband to the neck edge, enclosing the folded and basted end. Catch the end inside the fold. Pin and baste the 'V' down, past the staystitching. Machine-stitch just to the end of the 'V'.*

5 *Turn the neckband to the wrong side of the garment and hem all around just inside the seamline to finish the edge. Pin and catch down the unstitched edge of the band at the 'V' to prevent it from rolling.*

6 *The finished faced V-neckline has a sharp, overlapped point.*

Sleeves

THE NUMEROUS DIFFERENT STYLES OF SLEEVE are derived from only a few types of sleeve cap. The set-in sleeve, cut separately from the body of the garment, is the most versatile type of sleeve cap, and can be smooth, gathered or pleated. The raglan sleeve is also cut separately, but it has no cap. Instead, it continues smoothly over the shoulder to the neckline and becomes part of the upper bodice of the garment. All-in-one-sleeves, such as those used in kimonos, are not cut separately but are incorporated in the garment front and back pieces. In most dressmaking patterns, the sleeve cap has one notch in front and two at the back.

Gathered Sleeve

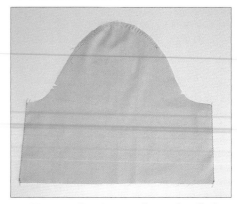

1 Cut out the pieces and transfer all the markings. After zigzagging the raw edges of the underarm seam, run a double row of gathering stitches between the two notches in each sleeve cap.

2 Stitch the underarm seam. Matching notches on the sleeve cap and the garment, pin the sleeve in place on the body of the garment. Draw up the gathers evenly between the notches.

3 Baste the sleeve cap to the garment, matching underarm seams and keeping gathers even over the shoulder area.

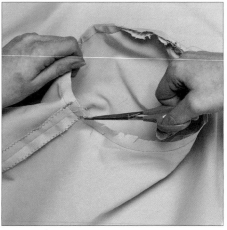

4 Stitch the sleeve seam. Zigzag around the raw edges 3/8 in (5mm) from the seam. Trim off excess fabric. Clip around the underarm, do not cut into the stitching.

USEFUL TIP

The raw edges of fabrics that fray easily, such as the terry towelling used here, can be bound all around with bias binding (see page 45) for a neat finish. This method not only protects the garment, preventing it from unravelling, but also makes it more comfortable to wear. Stitch a double seam around the armhole and trim the seam allowance to 3/8 in (5mm), then apply the binding.

Gathered sleeve

Pleated Sleeve

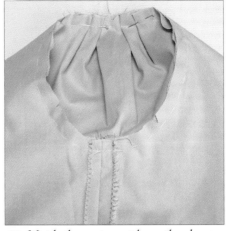

1 *Cut out, mark and prepare the sleeve as described in step 1 of the Gathered Sleeve, then stitch the underarm seam and zigzag the raw edges.*

2 *Match the center notch on the sleeve to the shoulder seam and follow the notches to make pleats, pinning each as you work. Baste, then stitch the seam. Finish as in step 4 of the Gathered Sleeve.*

Raglan Sleeve

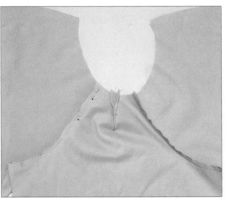

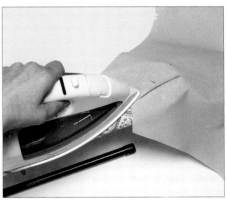

1 *Cut out and prepare the front, back and sleeve pieces, transferring markings and zigzagging the raw edges.*

2 *After stitching the sleeve cap dart, slash it open (see page 50, steps 5 and 6) and press flat. Repeat for the other sleeve. Matching notches, pin, baste and stitch the front and back sleeve seams.*

3 *After stitching, clip the curves, finish the raw edges with a zigzag stitch, and press the seams open.*

Pleated sleeve

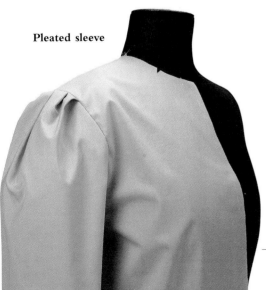

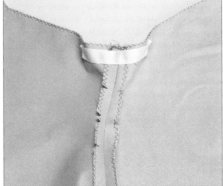

4 *Matching sleeve seams, pin, baste and stitch the underarm seams, catching in a 4 in (10 cm) length of seam tape across the seam, as shown, to reinforce it. Press the seam open.*

Raglan sleeve

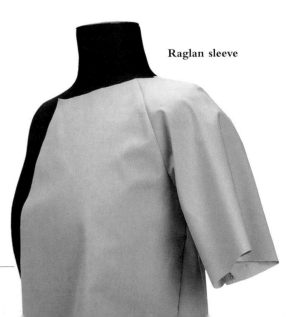

Cuffs and Plackets

Gathered and Ruffled Cuff

CUFFS ARE THE FINISHED ENDS OF SLEEVES. They can take many forms, from a simple turned-under hem to an elaborate lace frill. One of the simplest is a gathered cuff that incorporates a casing for elastic; this type of cuff can be finished with or without a frilly edge.

Cuffs that fit snugly at the wrist must have an opening slit that allows the hand to fit through, and this opening is called a placket. Plackets must be finished neatly as they are highly visible. They can be faced with a single piece of fabric or a bias-cut strip, or finished with two pieces of straight-cut binding to make a tailored placket.

Attaching a cuff to the end of a sleeve is similar to attaching a collar. It can be done before the sleeve is set in the garment if you are sure that the length of the sleeve is accurate.

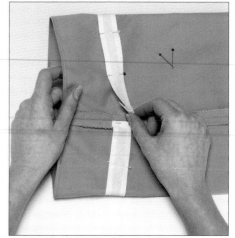

1 *Hem the edge of the sleeve, then measure up according to the depth of ruffle you desire. Pin seam tape or binding to the wrong side of the sleeve where you want the casing to be. Turn the short ends of the tape under where they meet at the underarm seam. Pin to secure.*

2 *Stitch both long edges of the tape to the sleeve. Thread a wrist-sized length of elastic through the opening in the casing. A safety pin attached to one end of the elastic helps guide it through.*

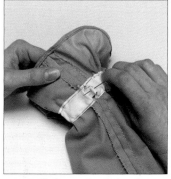

3 *Pull the ends of the elastic clear of the casing, overlap them and stitch together. Slipstitch the opening in the casing closed.*

4 *The finished cuff is neat and feminine. A similar cuff can be made by stitching rows of shirring elastic into the wrong side of the cuff. Shirring works well on delicate fabrics where a casing would show through.*

SIMPLE GATHERED CUFF

To create a gathered cuff without a frill, place one edge of binding right sides together on the raw edge of the sleeve end. Pin the short ends of the tape at the sleeve seam and stitch the casing along the long edge. Turn the binding to the wrong side and stitch the other edge in place. Thread a suitable length of elastic through the open ends, overlapping and stitching the ends of the elastic to secure. Slipstitch the opening in the casing closed.

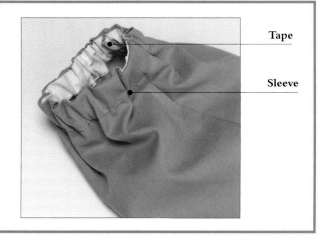

Tape

Sleeve

Faced Placket

1 *Cut out and prepare the sleeve and placket pieces. Pin together with right sides together, as shown above left. Stitch along the marked line, as shown above right. Using small, sharp scissors, slash between stitching lines to top of the 'V'.*

2 *Turn the placket piece to the wrong side and press. Topstitch around the 'V', as shown above left. The topstitching produces a neater overall finish, as shown above right, but it is not essential.*

Bias Placket

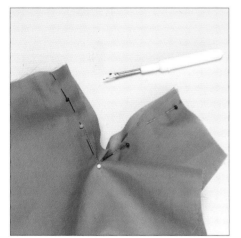

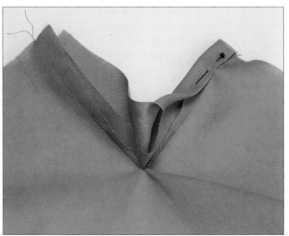

1 *After preparing sleeve and bias placket pieces, staystitch for 2 in (5 cm) on each side of the 'V', making a small horizontal stitch at the point. Using a seam ripper or small, sharp scissors, slash placket opening as far as the staystitching.*

2 *With right sides together, pin the bias piece to the placket. (The bottom edge of the sleeve is level with the corner of the placket. At the top, in the 'V', the placket is wider). Stitch the placket seam, turn the placket under to make a double fold and pin in place along the seam.*

3 *After stitching the placket in place, stitch a slanted seam across the top end, as shown, to neaten. This will help the placket lie flat once the cuff is attached.*

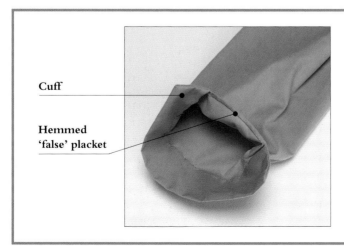

Cuff

Hemmed 'false' placket

HEMMED PLACKET

This 'false' placket is not a slit in the sleeve, but is produced from extra fabric allowed in the pattern at the end of the sleeve. Notches on the pattern indicate the placket area, which is turned over and hemmed before the cuff is attached. Hem this area and attach the cuff as in steps 1–3 of the Tailored Placket on page 58. This placket folds neatly when the cuff is buttoned.

Tailored Placket

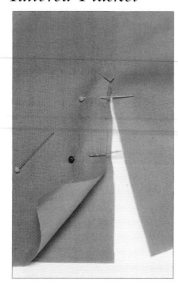

1 Cut out and prepare the sleeve piece and placket pieces. Cut an inverted 'V' shape at the top of the placket, as shown. Pin the right side of the smaller underlap placket piece to the wrong side of the sleeve.

2 After stitching the sleeve to the placket, turn under and press the seam allowance on the right side of the placket. Turn the placket to the right side of the sleeve and pin in place. Topstitch along the seamline.

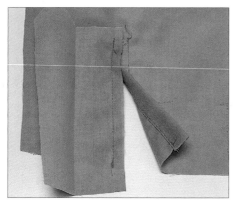

3 Place the right side of the larger overlap placket piece to the wrong side of the sleeve and pin. Stitch the seam, then press toward the overlap. Stitch the end of the overlap piece to the top edge of the slash. Press upward.

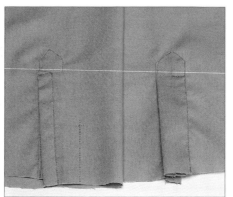

4 Turn under and press the seam allowance of the overlap placket, then tack. Fold to the right side, up to the stitching line, and pin. Topstitch along the fold to the top of the opening. Stitch the placket following the diagram (right).

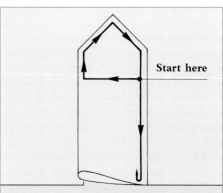

Start here

To secure all the layers, stitch across and up to the point of the placket, then down the side of the placket, following the direction of the arrows above. Stitch along the seamline to neaten.

Attaching Cuffs

1 These cuffs are ready to be attached. The top one is a single cuff, interfaced, folded and seamed along the short edges. The corners have been clipped. Below is a double or French cuff, twice the depth of the single cuff, shown turned right side out and pressed.

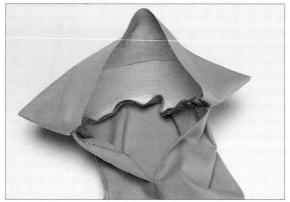

2 Attach one raw edge of the cuff to the right side of the sleeve along its raw edge. To do this, pin the cuff in place, easing in any fullness as instructed on the pattern, then baste and stitch the seam.

3 Turn the seam allowance of the remaining raw edge to the inside of the cuff and press. Pin in place and slipstitch by hand or topstitch by machine to finish.

Collars

COLLARS FINISH THE NECKLINE of many garments. There are many styles and sizes, from upright mandarin collars to flat-lying Peter Pan collars, but the construction of each type is similar. Most collars consist of two layers of fabric, with a layer of interfacing in between.

A collar is usually interfaced to give it body and shape. In addition, the interfacing helps to prevent the seam allowances inside the collar from showing through on the outside.

Simple Collar

1 *Assemble the garment front, back and facings, following the pattern instructions. Prepare the collar pieces as specified, and iron on or sew in any interfacings.*

2 *If the garment has lapels, fold and stitch this seam to finish the top fronts. Clip into the seam allowance at the end of the seam, as shown.*

3 *Stitch the seam to join the collar pieces. Trim excess seam allowance at the points by cutting out a triangle on each side, making sure you do not cut into the stitches. Turn right sides out and press.*

4 *Pin the raw edge of the collar to the neck edge of garment, matching notches carefully. Baste in place.*

5 *Pin and baste the facing in position and stitch the neck-edge seam together. Press the facing to the inside.*

Simple Collar
For added effect, topstitch a simple collar. Not only will the topstitching add a stylish decorative touch, but it will also keep the edges of the collar and garment front from rolling.

PETER PAN COLLAR

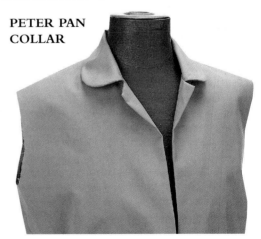

The method shown in steps 1–5, above can be used to apply a simple collar of any shape, such as the Peter Pan collar shown here. For instructions on clipping the curved seam, see page 39.

Shirt Collar

Also known as a stand collar, the collar on a 'man-tailored' shirt is effectively a simple collar combined with a Mandarin collar (see opposite). Although most often seen on men's shirts, this type of collar can also be used on women's garments and jackets. Topstitching can be added to this collar to emphasize the tailored effect.

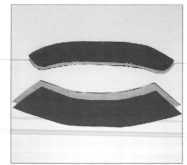

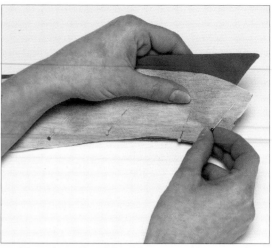

1 *After preparing and interfacing all the pieces of the garment and collar, interface one stand piece. Assemble the garment as necessary. Prepare and assemble the collar (see page 59), but not the stand piece.*

2 *Turn the collar right side out, making sure the corners are really sharp, and press. Pin, then baste and stitch the stand pieces to enclose the raw edge of the collar.*

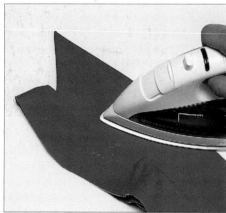

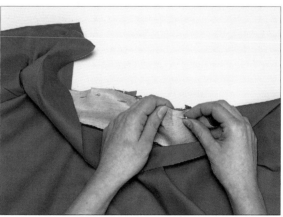

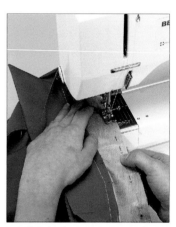

3 *After stitching, clip the curves as needed, then turn the stand and collar piece right sides out. Press along the seam.*

4 *Pin the right side of the interfaced raw edge of the stand to the right side of the neck edge of the garment, as shown.*

5 *Stitch the seam, removing the pins as you work. Finish as described in step 5 for the Simple Collar (page 59), then slipstitch inside the raw edge of the stand to cover the neckline seam.*

Shirt Collar
The combination of a simple collar with a stand piece creates a neatly tailored shirt.

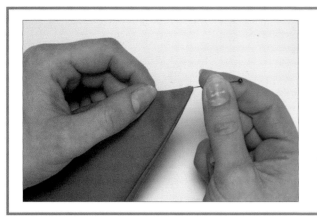

Mandarin Collar

A Mandarin collar stands up from the neckline seam. Widely used on Chinese garments, from which it takes its name, it is usually attached without facings.

1 *Follow steps 1 and 2 for the Simple Collar (page 59). Assemble the collar pieces and clip the seam allowance along the curves before pressing. Pin, baste and stitch, as shown for the simple collar.*

2 *Pin and stitch the interfaced layer of the collar to the neck edge. Clip the stitched seam and turn the collar right sides out.*

3 *Turn under the raw edge of the unstitched layer of the collar and pin it to enclose all layers of the seam.*

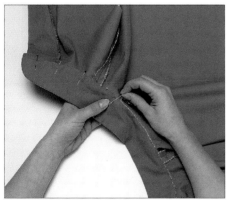

4 *Slipstitch the inside neck seam to make a neat finish. This method can be used to finish a collar on any garment that has no neck facings.*

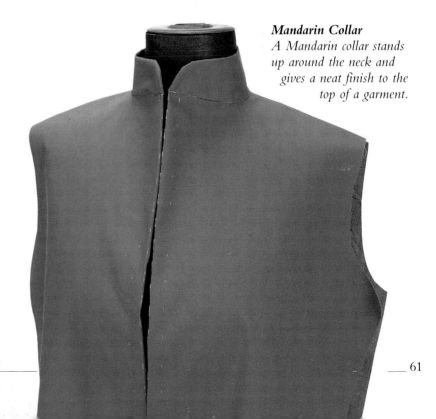

Mandarin Collar
A Mandarin collar stands up around the neck and gives a neat finish to the top of a garment.

Waistbands

WAISTBANDS ARE made from strips of fabric, usually the same fabric as the garment. These lengths are cut on the straight grain, interfaced and doubled. They finish the top raw edge of skirts or trousers, and are sometimes an integral part of dresses. A waistband can be narrow or wide, elasticized or held together with buttons or hooks and eyes. Instructions for assembling the waistband and a recommended closure are normally included in the pattern.

Simple Waistband

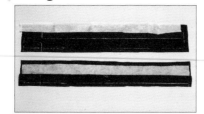

1 Cut out, mark and prepare the waistband piece and interfacing (top). Iron on or sew in the interfacing and press the center fold lengthwise (bottom).

2 Pin the waistband to the garment with right sides facing and matching openings. Inset: Stitch the seam, removing pins as you work. Stitch both short end seams and clip all four corners. For clarity, this garment is shown without a zip, which would normally be inserted before the waistband is attached.

3 Zigzag the unstitched edge, then turn the waistband right sides out. Pin in place and topstitch the long seam, working from the right side. Belt carrier loops can be added before the seam is stitched.

4 The waistband is shown from the wrong side. Hanging loops can be added, as here, by inserting an 8 in (20 cm) length of seam tape or ribbon at each side seam, catching it into the first long seam before stitching (see step 3).

FINISHING OFF

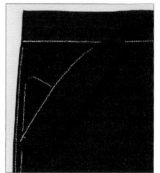

On light- or medium-weight fabrics, you can finish the waistband by turning it right sides out and turning the raw edge under, before topstitching as in step 3. Catch in any belt loops and hanging loops.

USEFUL TIP

Grading seams on thick fabrics will help to reduce bulk. After stitching the seam, trim the allowance 1/8 in (3 mm) from the stitching on the top layer of fabric, then trim 1/4 in (5 mm) from stitching on the next layer, continuing as necessary to layer the seam allowance as shown.

Stiffened Waistband

1 Prepare the waistband piece as in step 1 above, cutting grosgrain (petersham ribbon) for a stiffer finish. Pin and stitch both long edges of grosgrain (petersham) in place along one side of the waistband.

2 Stitch the waistband to the garment, as in step 2 above. Turn to the inside with the raw edge folded under. Pin and topstitch the long edge. Fold the short ends inside, pin and slipstitch to finish.

Elastic Waistband with Separate Gathered Casing

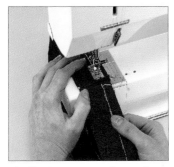

1 *Baste seams on long edges of casing. Stitch long edges, wrong sides together, turning in seam allowances at the gap in the center seam.*

2 *Join the seams of the garment. Run two rows of gathering stitches along the top edge of the garment and carefully pull up the gathers.*

3 *With right sides together, pin the raw edge of the waistband casing to the top gathered edge of the garment, matching center seamlines and distributing the gathers in the skirt evenly as you pin. Stitch the band in place, removing the pins as you work.*

4 *Thread a length of elastic through the casing, as in step 1 of the Folded Casing, below. Stitch across the elastic by hand to secure. Slipstitch the gap in the casing closed.*

TECHNIQUES	page
Basting	33
Gathering	35
Marking	27
Understanding patterns	24

USEFUL TIP

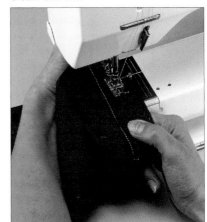

To secure elastic and distribute gathers evenly at the same time, zigzag along the center of the waistband. Pull the elastic gently to keep the casing fabric smooth as you work. Stitch more than one row, if you wish.

Elastic Waistband with Folded Casing

1 *Mark the depth of waistband desired. Turn raw edge under ¼ in (5 mm). Fold over to make a casing, pin and topstitch, leaving a gap at one side seam. Thread elastic through, overlap the ends and stitch through the layers to secure.*

2 *Close the gap for the elastic in the folded casing by continuing the topstitching across the seam.*

DRAWSTRING WAISTBAND

Make a folded casing, as shown left, leaving a gap in the right side of the center seam in the garment. Thread through a suitable length of cord. This waistband is especially useful for pajamas and sports clothes.

Hems

Simple Hand-stitched Hem

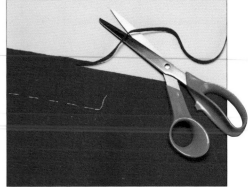

HEMS ARE USED TO FINISH THE BOTTOM of garments and the edges of simple sleeves, as well as the edges of such home furnishings as tablecloths, bedspreads and curtains. There are several methods for working hems, depending on the style of the garment or furnishing accessory, the weight of the fabric and the desired look.

Hems can be worked by hand or stitched on the machine, and in most cases should be virtually invisible. The usual way of making a hem is to turn under a narrow edge, and then turn the edge under again to enclose the raw edge completely. On heavyweight fabrics, or where there is not enough fabric to turn a hem, the edge can be faced or bound. All hems can be basted in place to help ensure accuracy, but pinning is usually enough.

1 *Mark top and bottom of the hem by folding and pressing the fabric, and baste along the bottom foldline. Trim raw edge to 1/4 in (5 mm) of the first fold.*

2 *Turn up and press the bottom foldline. Baste along the top marked line and through the center of the turned-up fold, making sure all seams match.*

3 *Turn under the top fold along the basted line and pin the hem in place. You can now sew the hem.*

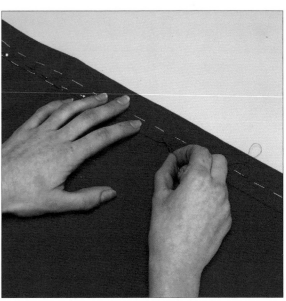

4 *To work a tailor's hem, place the fabric wrong side up on a flat surface. Pick up 1 or 2 threads at a time while taking the needle through the edge of the top fold, removing pins as you work. When hemming is completed, remove all basting stitches.*

TYPES OF HAND-SEWN HEMS

There are many ways of working a hand-sewn hem, and you may like to experiment with a few different techniques to decide which one you prefer.

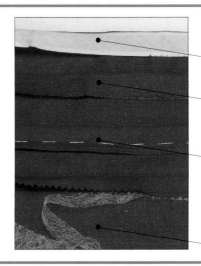

Bias or straight binding is machine-stitched to the raw edge of a levelled hem, then turned up and pressed, and then hand- or machine-stitched in place.

The raw edge is zigzagged, then turned up. The hem is herringbone-stitched in place.

On lightweight fabric, the raw edge is turned under and machine-stitched, folded up and basted, and then sewn with a tailor's hem, as described in step 4 above.

Fusible hem tape is good for emergency repairs and can be used on lightweight fabrics, though it may work loose during laundering. Here the raw edge has been pinked and turned up, and the tape inserted into the fold and pressed in place.

HAND STITCHES

Slant Hemming *is used on garments and home furnishings that need a fine hem. Take the needle in at a seam and fasten off. Take small, evenly spaced stitches along the top edge of the hem.*

Vertical Hemming *is easier to work on heavier fabrics. Start off as for slant hemming, but keep the stitches upright. Make sure that the stitches on the right side of the garment are as small as possible.*

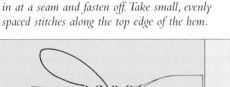

Blind Hemming *makes an invisible hem. Finish the raw edge. Take a tiny stitch on the wrong side, then pick up one garment thread. Hold the edge down and pick up stitches on each side of the hem.*

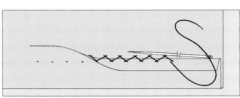

Blind Herringbone *is useful for knitted fabrics. Tiny stitches are picked up first on the wrong side, then on the garment, as for blind hemming, but it is worked like herringbone stitch (see page 33).*

Trouser Turn-up

1 *With trouser leg wrong side out, fold and baste 3 lines – bottom edge of turn-up (bottom line), top of turn-up (center line), and trouser hemline (top line). Zigzag raw edge. Turn up the center fold and press. Secure zigzagged raw edge with herringbone stitch.*

2 *Turn trouser leg right side out. Turn up bottom fold and press. Turn under top fold and press. Catchstitch at the seams to secure. Remove the basting.*

Curved Hem

1 *Carefully mark and cut the hem. Zigzag the raw edge and baste the foldline. Run a row of gathering stitches 1/4 in (5 mm) from the zigzagging.*

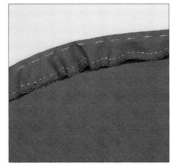

2 *Turn up the hem along the tacked foldline. Baste the hem in place about 1/4 in (5 mm) from the fold.*

3 *Matching the seams, pin the hem in place, pulling up the gathering thread as you work to spread the fabric evenly and ease in fullness.*

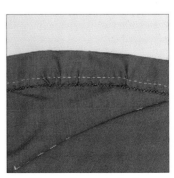

4 *Herringbone-stitch the hem in place from the wrong side, removing pins as you work. Remove all basting and press.*

Simple Machine-stitched Hem

1 Measure, mark and baste two foldlines, the first 1/4 in (5 mm) from the raw edge and the second 1/2 in (1.25 cm) from the first. Turn the first fold under and press.

2 Turn the second fold under and press. Pin the double-folded hem in place, matching seams.

3 On the wrong side of the fabric, stitch along the top fold, removing pins as you work. Remove the basting and press the hem.

Topstitched Hem

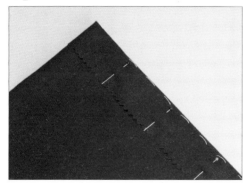

TWIN-NEEDLE TOPSTITCHING

1 After measuring and marking the hem, and basting the foldline, pink the raw edge. Turn the hem under at the foldline and pin in place, matching seams.

2 Working on the right side of fabric, topstitch the hem. Follow the guidelines marked on the machine plate for accuracy. Remove the basting and press.

For an attractive neat finish to a topstitched hem, use a twin needle to topstitch. Alternatively, work two rows of topstitching side by side.

Machine-Stitched Blind-hem

Using a special blind-hemming guide attachment, available for most modern sewing machines, it is possible to stitch a blind hem that is suitable for almost any fabric, but particularly useful on heavyweight fabrics and knits.

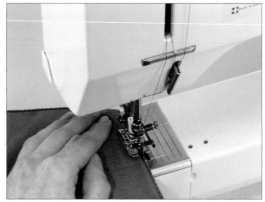

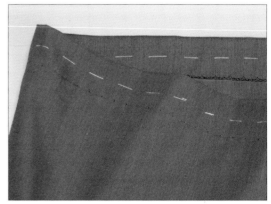

1 Mark the hem. Zigzag the raw edge. Fold the hem under and baste in place about 1/4 in (5 mm) from the zigzagged edge. Fold hem to right side of garment along basting line and stitch using a blind-hemming attachment.

2 The straight stitches follow the edge of the hem while the pointed stitches catch the fabric on the right side to make a strong hem that is virtually invisible from the right side of the garment.

Faced Hem

1 Mark the hemline on the raw edge. Cut a facing strip measuring 1½ in (3 cm) wide and the length of the hem, plus seam allowances. Fold under and press ¼ in (5 mm) on both long edges.

2 Fold under the short ends. Matching one short end to the garment seam, as shown, and with right sides facing, pin a folded long edge of the facing to the garment along the marked hemline.

3 Stitch the seam, removing pins as you work. Overlap the final short end over the sewn folded end, as shown, and finish stitching. Turn the facing to the wrong side of the garment and press the seam.

4 Make sure the raw edge of the facing is turned under, and then pin the facing in place.

5 Hem along the top edge of the facing by hand, as shown. Press again to finish.

BOUND HEM

This hem is similar in construction to the faced hem, above, but uses a length of bias binding instead of a straight strip of fabric. It is useful for curved hems, and can be turned back as an invisible facing or used as a decorative feature.

If you wish to coordinate the binding to the garment or accessory and cannot find a ready-made bias binding of the correct color or width, you can make your own bias binding using the same fabric by following the instructions on pages 44–5.

 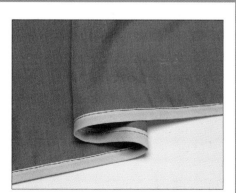

1 Mark and pin the hem as described in step 2 of the Faced Hem. Stitch the binding to the garment's raw edge.

2 Turn the binding under and topstitch along the top fold of the binding on the right side, as shown.

ROLLED HEMS

Rolled hems can be sewn by hand or machine. A fine hem that is first rolled and then stitched by hand is traditionally the finest finish possible on delicate fabrics that fray easily, such as silk, organdy or chiffon. It is worked mainly on scarves and formal dresses.

Machine-rolled hems provide a stronger and sharper finish. They are acceptable for garments made from lightweight fabrics, and are also quicker to work. The first of the two methods shown here also applies to hems on medium-weight and heavier fabrics, but the hem would normally be deeper than the one shown. The second method takes less time, but requires a steady cutting hand. It is finished with a double row of stitching – shown here as two separate lines, but which can be worked on top of one another for a neater finish.

Hand-rolled Hem

1 *Cut the raw edge of the fabric straight, trimming away a little at a time as you work. You may want to mark the hemline with a fine pencil before you cut the fabric.*

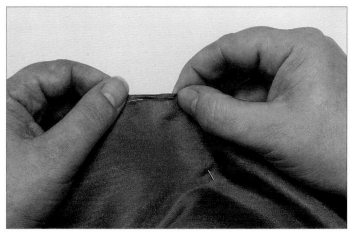

2 *Carefully roll the cut edge inward, enclosing the raw fabric completely. Again, work on a small area at a time and keep the roll small – the smaller the roll, the finer the hem.*

3 *Holding the rolled edge tightly over one finger, take two or three evenly spaced stitches onto the needle, picking up only a thread at a time if possible. Pull the stitches gently and repeat.*

4 *A hand-rolled hem should be neat on both sides with evenly spaced stitches. In order to make a sharp, neat corner, clip a small triangle, and then turn and miter it carefully (see page 41). If necessary, use a fine pin to hold it in place as you work.*

Method 1 – Machine-rolled Hem

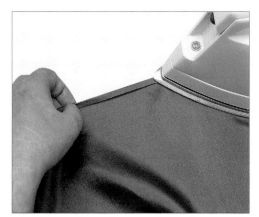  

1 Turn under and press a hem of an appropriate width along the edge to be hemmed. Then turn and press a double hem.

2 Pin the pressed hem in place, matching seams. Position the pins parallel to the edge of the hem, pointing to the left. Baste the hem in place around the corners.

3 Working with the wrong side up, machine-stitch the hem. Remove each pin carefully as you come to it. Press the hem to finish.

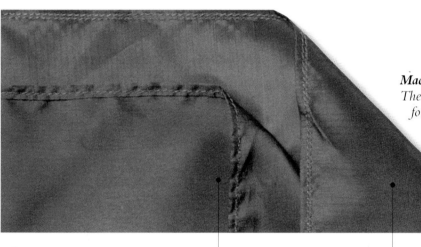

Hem made by Method 1   Hem made by Method 2

Machine-rolled Hems

The two hems shown here are straightforward and useful for sheer and lightweight fabric. Method 2 is also good for hemming ruffles. The Method 1 example, left, creates a more obvious hem than the hem using Method 2, which looks double-sided. It is difficult to identify the wrong side of the fabric in the Method 2 example. If the hem is cut on the bias, do not press before stitching as it will stretch. Turn under and baste.

Method 2 – Machine-rolled Hem

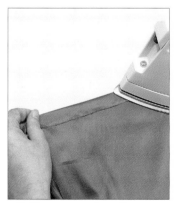 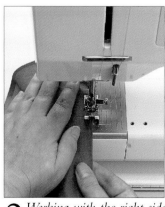  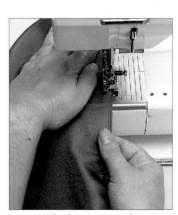

1 Press a turning of approximately 3/4 in (1.5 cm) to the wrong side of the fabric.

2 Working with the right side up, machine stitch 1/4 in (5 mm) from the fold.

3 Hold the stitching line open, as shown, and use small, very sharp scissors to trim the excess fabric as close to the stitches as possible.

4 With the wrong side up, and working as close as you can to the stitching line, make another straight line of stitching to prevent the raw edge from fraying.

Pockets

POCKETS ARE AN INTEGRAL part of many
garments and can also provide a strong
decorative feature. They are usually made
in the same fabric as the garment, but in
garments made from heavyweight fabrics,
such as wool or corduroy, internal pockets are
generally made from material that is lighter in
weight. Pockets should always be strong
enough to withstand normal wear and tear.
There are several different types, such as
patch pockets, in-seam, front hip and welt,
each with their own specific technique.

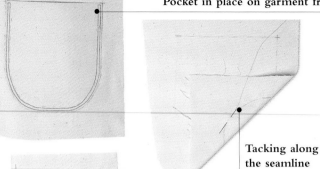

Pocket in place on garment front

Tacking along the seamline

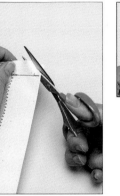

Marked pocket piece

Patch Pockets

Patch pockets are placed on the
outside of a garment. They are
the simplest pockets to construct
and have many variations. Corners
can be squared or rounded, and the
pockets can be made from fabric that
contrasts with or matches the garment
fabric. They can be unlined, lined or
self-lined by doubling the fabric.

Basic Patch Pocket

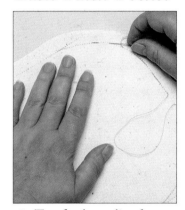

1 Transfer the outline from
the pattern to the wrong
side of the garment and pocket
pieces. Cut out and baste along
the pocket seamline. Zigzag
along the top raw edge.

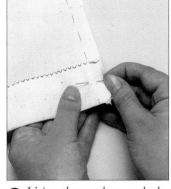

2 Using the notches marked
on the pattern for
positioning, fold right sides
together along the top edge
and pin in place.

3 Machine-stitch each end of
the fold from the zigzag
stitching to the folded edge.
Carefully clip the top corners
of the pocket, as shown.

4 Turn the top of the pocket
inside out. To make the
corner sharp and square, use
a pin to tease it out once you
have turned the top edge to
the right side.

5 Turn and press the pocket
edge to the wrong side
along the lines basted in step
1. Pin and baste in place,
easing the curves gently.

6 The pocket is now ready to
apply to the basted outline
on the garment. The final
stitching that secures its shape
also anchors it to the garment.

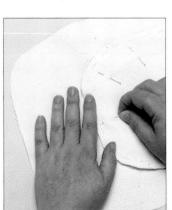

7 Pin the pocket in position
on the garment along the
basted outline. The pocket is
now ready to be stitched on.

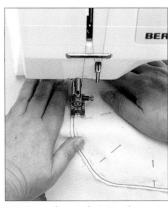

8 Sew the pocket in place
with a double row of
topstitching. Decorative triangles
can be stitched at each end
of the seam.

Lined Patch Pocket

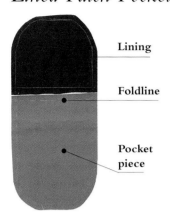

- Lining
- Foldline
- Pocket piece

1 *Cut out the pocket and lining. Mark the seam allowances with a row of basting stitches.*

2 *With right sides together, pin, baste and stitch the top-edge seam. Note that the lining piece is shorter than the pocket piece.*

3 *Press the seam toward the bottom of the pocket. Press the top crease. The pocket is now doubled.*

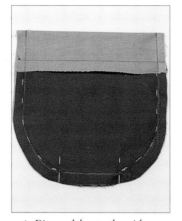

4 *Pin and baste the sides and bottom of the pocket, leaving a gap for turning the pocket right sides out.*

5 *Turn the pocket right sides out through the gap.*

6 *Baste all around the edge, closing the gap as you work. Stitch the pocket to the garment, following steps 7 and 8 for the Patch Pocket.*

SELF-LINED PATCH POCKET

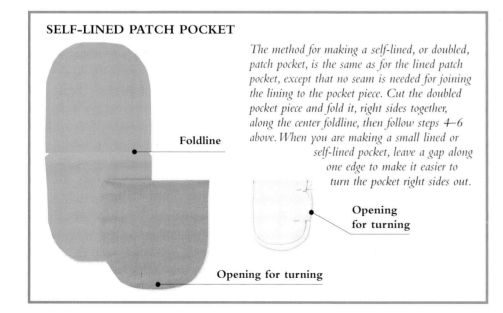

- Foldline
- Opening for turning
- Opening for turning

The method for making a self-lined, or doubled, patch pocket, is the same as for the lined patch pocket, except that no seam is needed for joining the lining to the pocket piece. Cut the doubled pocket piece and fold it, right sides together, along the center foldline, then follow steps 4–6 above. When you are making a small lined or self-lined pocket, leave a gap along one edge to make it easier to turn the pocket right sides out.

Decorative Effects
Pockets can be trimmed and decorated in an infinite variety of ways. This pocket for a child's garment uses braid edging and an iron-on motif.

Magic Pocket

This clever technique, which works best on fairly large pockets, is sewn so no stitching lines are apparent, yet is essentially a patch pocket.

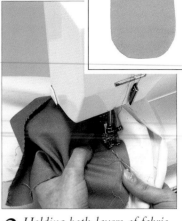

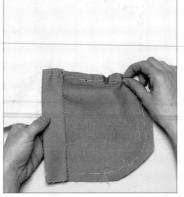

1 *Cut out the pieces. Using dressmaker's carbon, mark the position of the pocket on the garment and the seamline on the pocket. Baste the seamline. Matching basting, place a carbon face down on the right side of the garment. Place another carbon face up and position the wrong side of the pocket on top. Mark a series of identical balance marks on both garment and pocket.*

2 *Turn under, pin and stitch a double hem at the top of the pocket. Matching basted seamlines and the positional balance marks, pin right sides together along one side.*

3 *Holding both layers of fabric taut, stitch along the seamline. Remove each pin as you work, and reposition it further along the seamline. Inset: The pocket does not have any visible seams or topstitching.*

Front Hip Pocket

These pockets are usually found on skirts and trousers, and are attached at the waist and side seams of the garment. The pockets are made up of a front piece that needs to be the same fabric as the garment and a backing or facing piece, which may be a lining fabric. Here the dark piece is the pocket front.

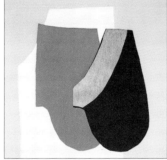

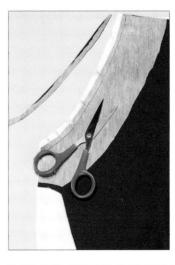

1 *Cut out and mark garment and pocket pieces. Iron or sew interfacing to the wrong side edge of pocket front piece.*

2 *With right sides together, pin and stitch the pocket front piece to the garment front. Grade (see page 62) and clip the seam allowance.*

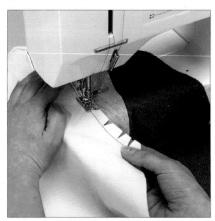

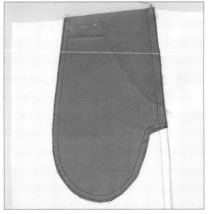

3 *Neatly staystitch the inside seam allowance along the clipped seam edge to reinforce the curve. This 'understitched' line will appear as a topstitched line on the inside edge of the finished pocket.*

4 *Press and baste the curved seam. Pin and stitch the pocket back to the pocket front along the curves. Zigzag the raw edges.*

5 *Pin and stitch the garment side seam and finish the raw edges by zigzagging. Press to one side so the pocket lies flat against garment front. Baste in position along the waist and side seams, as shown.*

6 *The finished front hip pocket, shown in a contrasting fabric for clarity, lies smoothly along the hip line of the garment.*

Side Seam Pocket

Also called an in-seam pocket, this type lies inside the seam of the garment, usually at the side. Side seam pockets are widely used in skirts, dresses and trousers, and are frequently found in jackets and coats. They are often made in a lighter weight of fabric to reduce bulk, especially on outdoor wear and trousers.

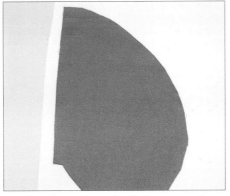

1 Cut out and mark all the pieces. Cut two pieces of seam tape slightly longer than the pocket opening. These will be used to reinforce the pocket edge.

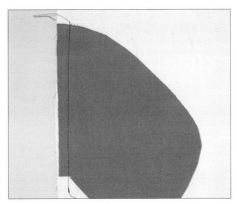

2 With wrong sides together and matching raw edges, pin and stitch the pocket to the seam allowance of the garment. Stitch a length of seam tape along the seam on the wrong side of the garment. Repeat the process for the second pocket.

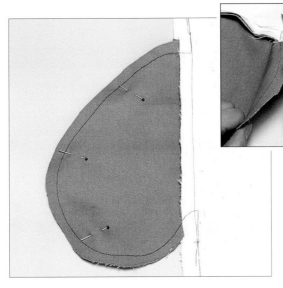

3 With right sides together, pin the garment sides and pocket pieces together. Stitch down the garment seam and around the curve of the pocket, backstitching at the top and bottom of the pocket to strengthen the joins. Inset: Clip at the joins.

4 Press the side seams of the garment open. This pocket is a virtually invisible slit in the right side of the seam.

SIDE SEAM ALTERNATIVES

Patterns give in-seam pockets in a variety of ways. Some are attached to a self-facing pocket edge that is cut in one piece with the garment piece. Other versions are cut with the garment as an integrated piece. Both types are assembled using the method shown.

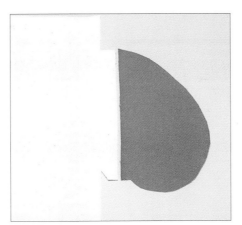

Above: This method of making an in-seam pocket is used mainly on heavy fabrics in which a lighter-weight pocket is needed. The facing strip keeps the line of the garment smooth and the pocket remains invisible.

Above: All-in-one side seam pockets can be used for lightweight or medium-weight fabrics. It is important to strengthen them with backstitching where they join the side seams, as in step 3 above.

Welted Pocket

Welts are strips of fabric used on edges of pockets to strengthen them and add a tailored finish. Precision in measuring and marking is vital when making any of the welted pockets shown here. To reduce bulk, cut the pocket from from lining fabric. Cut the pocket back, which will be seen through the pocket opening, from garment fabric. Basting, both to mark positions and to secure the work at various stages, is essential.

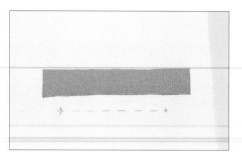

1 Cut out all the pieces. Mark and baste the pocket position on the garment. Fold both welt pieces in half lengthwise and press.

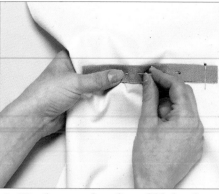

2 Pin the raw edge of one folded welt piece to the top of the basted line on the garment piece. Repeat with the second welt piece, pinning it below the basted line.

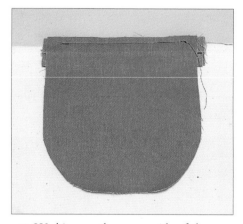

3 Stitch both welt pieces in place along the long edges. Do not stitch across the short ends of the welt pieces.

4 Using small, sharp scissors, slash the pocket slit from right side, leaving 1/2 in (1.25 cm) uncut at each end. Clip into each corner of the slash, as shown. Inset: Turn back a triangle at each end of the slash and baste and stitch on wrong side.

5 Turn the welts to the wrong side through the slit to finish the right side edges. Baste the finished edges of the welt together to reinforce them. Do not remove the basting until the garment has been completed.

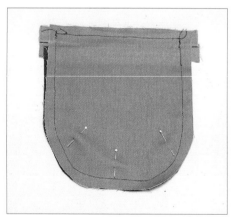

6 Working on the wrong side of the garment, match the top edge of the pocket piece to the raw edge of the top welt. Pin and stitch in place, folding the garment piece out of the way to avoid stitching through it by mistake.

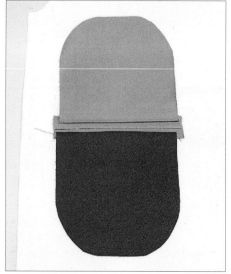

7 Attach the second pocket piece to the bottom welt, as described in step 6. Fold the top pocket piece down and press.

8 Pin the two pocket pieces together and stitch along the curve of the pocket. Finish the raw edges with zigzagging.

Single Welt Pocket

Unlike the basic welted pocket, which uses two strips of fabric to make the welt, this pocket uses a single strip to cover the edge of the pocket opening. The pocket is cut in one piece, unlike the welted and bound pockets which are cut as two pieces, and can be made from lining fabric to reduce bulk.

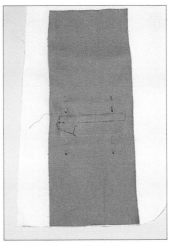

1 Mark the pocket position on the garment piece. Fold and press the welt lengthwise. With right sides together, stitch the short edges. Turn out, press, then baste the welt to the lower edge of the marked seamline on the right side of garment piece.

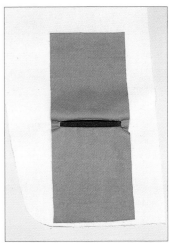

2 Pin the pocket piece over the welt on the right side of the garment. Stitch all four edges of the marked line.

3 Cut a slit in the pocket piece as described in steps 4 and 5 of the Welted Pocket. Pull the pocket through to the wrong side of the garment.

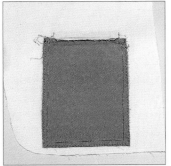

4 Pin the pocket pieces together and stitch to finish as described in step 8 of the Welted Pocket.

5 The welt stays on the right side of the garment. Topstitch the ends of the welt to secure it to the garment.

FALSE POCKET

To make a false pocket, or cover a plain slit pocket, cut two pieces in the shape of the pocket flap. With right sides together, pin and stitch all sides except the top side. Notch corners and turn right side out. If desired, topstitch edges. Position the right side of flap upside-down on the garment, then fold over to cover the raw edge and pin in place. Topstitch flap to the garment piece.

Bound Pocket

A bound pocket is made in the same way as a bound buttonhole (see page 79), with a single strip of fabric covering the raw edges of the pocket opening.

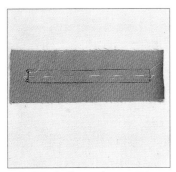

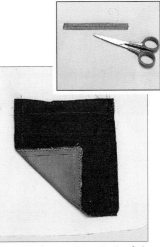

1 Mark the pocket position on the garment piece and baste stitching lines on the pocket piece. With right sides together, baste and stitch the pocket to the garment, around all four basted edges.

2 Slash through the pocket, as described in steps 4–5 of the Welted Pocket.

3 Turn the pocket patch through the slit to the wrong side of the garment. Press, then baste the slit closed. Stitch a pocket piece to each long raw edge of the binding patch.

4 Refer to steps 6–8 of the Welted Pocket to attach the pocket pieces at the top and bottom edges of the welt. Inset: Stitch the pocket edges together and zigzag raw edges.

Zippers

MOST GARMENTS, AND MANY home furnishing items, need some form of fastener. Zippers, perhaps the most daunting fastener to insert, consist of a fabric tape held together by a set of metal or plastic teeth that interlock when a slider is pulled. Different types and weights are available; always choose the one suitable for your style of garment and weight of fabric.

Center Zippers

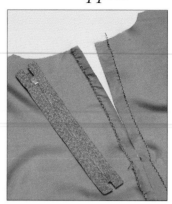

1 *Measure and mark the position for the zipper on the seams, using the zipper as a guide. Stitch the seam up to the markings, being sure to leave enough room at the top for the facing seam. Finish the raw edges with zigzag stitch. A plastic zipper has been used here, which is more appropriate than a metal one for this lightweight fabric.*

2 *Place the closed zipper on the center seam and pin it in the correct position. Baste the zipper in place.*

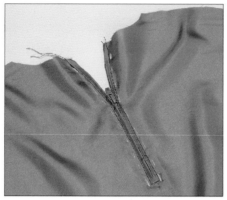

3 *Turn the garment to the right side. Starting at one top edge and working around to the other, stitch the zipper in place using a zipper foot. Make sure that the corners are neat and square.*

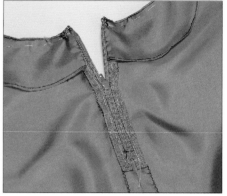

4 *Add the facing (see page 52), or the waistband if making a skirt or trousers, and slipstitch the ends to the zipper tape. Keep the stitches clear of the teeth. Add additional fasteners, as desired, and then remove the basting.*

Lapped Zipper

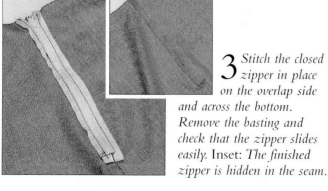

1 *Stitch the seam, ending at the point where the zipper will begin. Finish the raw edges. Open the zipper, then pin and baste it to one side of the seam allowance, which will be the underlap side. Working from the wrong side, use a zipper foot to stitch it in place. Inset: Move the slider clear of the foot as you work. Stitch a length of seam tape to the finished raw edge of the overlap side of the seam allowance to strengthen it.*

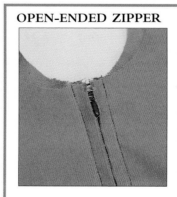

2 *Fold the overlap edge to the wrong side, then pin and baste the closed zipper in place.*

3 *Stitch the closed zipper in place on the overlap side and across the bottom. Remove the basting and check that the zipper slides easily. Inset: The finished zipper is hidden in the seam.*

OPEN-ENDED ZIPPER

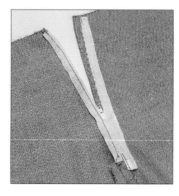

To insert an open-ended zipper in a jacket or waistcoat, fold the lengthwise facings or seam allowances under and baste along the seamline. Insert the zipper as shown for center zippers, stitching on the right side of the garment. Remove all basting stitches and make sure the zipper slides easily.

Fly Front Zipper

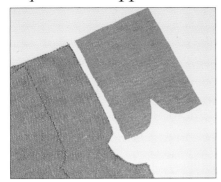

1 *Cut out and prepare all the garment pieces. Finish the raw edges and baste all zipper markings shown on the pattern.*

2 *Fold the fly piece in half and topstitch ⅛ in (3 mm) from the fold. Zigzag stitch all other edges together to secure them. Stitch curved garment seam, backstitching a few times at each end. Fold the underlap to the wrong side and baste along the fold.*

• • • • • • • • • • • • •

TECHNIQUES   page
Basting   **33**
Understanding
patterns   **24**

3 *Open the zipper. Aligning the teeth with the edge of underlap fold, pin, baste and stitch the zipper in place on the underlap side. Inset: Close the zipper and fold the overlap along the basted line, then baste in place. Baste through all layers on the overlap side.*

4 *Pin the fly piece over the closed zipper, matching its curved edge with the curved edge of the underlap. Baste in place along the seamline.*

5 *Working on the right side of the garment, follow the curved line of basting to make a double row of topstitching.*

6 *Remove all basting stitches. The double row of stitching strengthens the curve on the finished fly, shown here on the wrong side.*

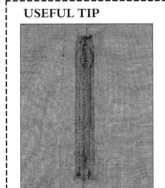

USEFUL TIP

To shorten a zipper, sew the bar half of a hook and bar fastening across the point where you want the zipper to end. Cut the end of the zipper below the bar. This method can also be used to finish lengths of zipper tape bought by the yard (meter).

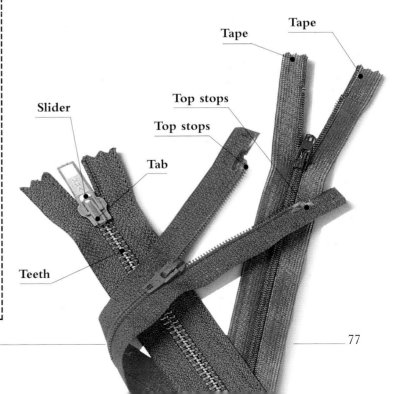

Buttons and Buttonholes

BUTTONS ARE AVAILABLE in almost any size and shape imaginable. Buttonholes can be as simple as a hole cut in fabric with the raw edges hand-stitched, or as complicated as a bound buttonhole. Other fasteners, such as hooks and eyes, can also be used for closures.

Hand-sewn Buttonhole

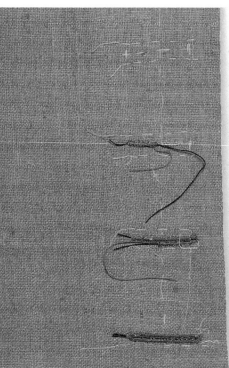

1 Mark the buttonhole position on the wrong side of the buttonhole band. Baste to mark the center line. Baste along each long side to stabilize the buttonhole.

2 Slit the center. Cut waxed thread to more than twice the buttonhole length. Lay thread on top edge and work buttonhole stitch (see page 33) over edge, catching in the cord.

3 Repeat along the lower edge of the buttonhole, continuing to catch in the cord as you work around.

4 Catch down the cord at the end with a few straight stitches. Trim the ends of the cord. Remove basting.

Machine-worked Buttonhole

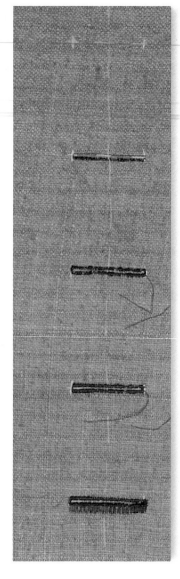

1 Mark the buttonhole on the back of the buttonhole band. Baste through to the right side to mark the center and each end.

2 Run a straight line of machine stitching above and below the basted center line. Work a row of tight satin stitch (see page 35) along one row of the straight stitching.

3 Take several long stitches at each end of the buttonhole. Cover the second line of straight stitches with satin stitch, as in step 2.

4 Repeat steps 2 and 3 to strengthen and finish. Remove the basting. Starting in the center and working first to one end and then the other, use a seam ripper to slit open the buttonhole. Take care not to cut the stitching.

Zigzag Finish
Adding extra-wide zigzag stitches to one or both edges of the finished buttonhole strengthens the opening.

USEFUL TIP

To position a button accurately, place the button band and the buttonhole band together and insert a pin through the center of the buttonhole. Sew on the button at the pinned point.

Always make a test buttonhole on a scrap of fabric to check the size before working the buttonholes in your garment.

Sewing on Buttons

From the top: A four-hole and a two-hole button are sewn by taking the needle in the hole, through the fabric and back through the hole from the other side. A shank button stands above the surface of the fabric. To make a thread shank, cross pins between button and fabric and attach button, winding thread around the needles between each stitch. To attach military-style buttons with a metal pin, make a hole in the button position and buttonhole stitch around it to prevent fraying; unclip pin, insert shank in hole and clip pin back on button on wrong side.

Other Fasteners

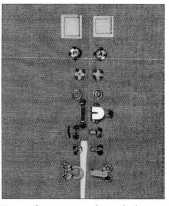

From the top: touch-and-close tape; metal popper snap; plastic popper snap; punch-in metal popper snap; heavy-duty hook and bar; lightweight hook and bar; lightweight hook and eye; thread-wrapped hook and eye.

Bound Buttonholes

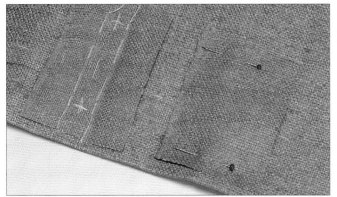

1 Mark the buttonholes on the wrong side of the band. With right sides together, pin a fabric patch, measuring about 1 in (2.5 cm) wider and longer than the buttonhole, centrally, as shown right. Mark the center and ends with basting. Baste a line 1/8 in (3 mm) away from the center on each side.

2 Next, fold the square of fabric up along the basted lines on each side as shown. Then baste again to secure in place. Stitch along each basted line.

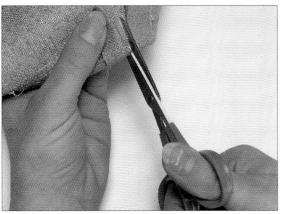

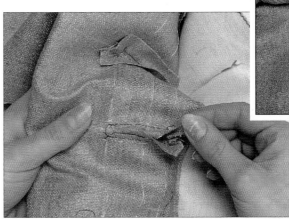

3 Turn the stitched edges back. Fold the buttonhole in half, matching the ends. Use scissors to cut carefully along the center basted line. Clip a small triangle into the corners at each end (see step 4).

4 Now pull the buttonhole square through to the wrong side of the garment. Press carefully and baste the opening closed. Inset: Turn back each short end and stitch down to secure the tiny triangle piece to the patch, making sure you do not stitch it to the garment.

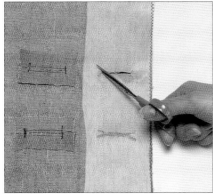

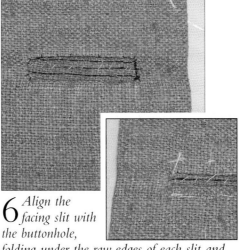

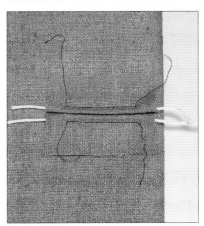

5 Slit each buttonhole position in the facing, starting from the center and clipping a triangle in each end, as shown (see page 74, see step 4).

6 Align the facing slit with the buttonhole, folding under the raw edges of each slit and pinning. Hand-stitch the facing to the patch only. Inset: The stitching lines do not appear on the right side of the garment. Repeat the steps to make all the buttonholes, then remove the basting.

CORDED BUTTONHOLES

To make corded buttonholes, prepare as for step 1 of Bound Buttonholes, above, then slip a length of cord under each folded edge in step 2. Stitch in place, then proceed as for steps 3–6.

Linings

MANY GARMENTS ARE lined to give shape and protect seams and raw edges. Because a lining increases the thickness of the garment, lining fabric is usually lightweight. Linings can be joined to the garment at the top and left unsecured at the bottom – usually seen on skirts or trousers – or sewn into the garment all around, as in a jacket. Most linings are assembled in the same way as the garment and then sewn in just before the garment is completed. You may like to hem the lining before attaching it, but for a full-length lining, hem the lining when you hem the garment.

Lining a Skirt

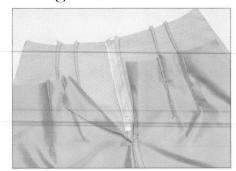

1 *Assemble the skirt and lining pieces, aligning the zipper with the seam in the lining. The corresponding seam in the lining should be open from the waist to the bottom of the zipper.*

2 *Matching darts and with wrong sides together, pin and baste the skirt and lining pieces along the waist. Fold under the seam allowance on the open seam of the lining piece, then pin and baste in place around the zipper.*

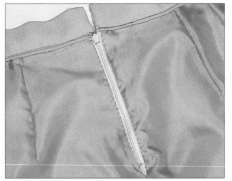

3 *Slipstitch the lining to the zipper tape. Do not sew through to the right side of the skirt. Finally attach the waistband to the skirt (see page 62).*

Lining a Waistcoat

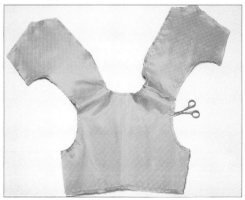

1 *Join center back and shoulder seams on the garment and lining pieces. With right sides together and matching seams, pin and baste lining to waistcoat. Stitch all edges except four side seams under armholes. Trim and clip curved seams and cut off points.*

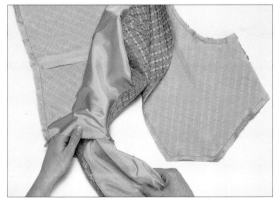

2 *Pull the waistcoat right sides out through the open side seams. Press carefully, paying particular attention to the edges.*

3 *With the lining side seams pinned out of the way, pin and stitch the side seams of the garment, right sides together. Press.*

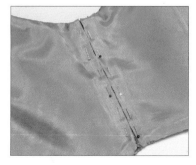

4 *Fold under the seam allowance on each side seam in the lining and pin it in place. Slipstitch, catching the seam allowance on the garment, but do not sew through to the right side of the waistcoat. Press to finish.*

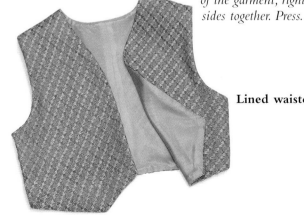

Lined waistcoat

Finishing the Bottom Edge

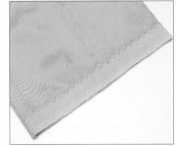

Split Skirt
Leave the bottom of the center seam on the lining open. Clip the seam allowance at the top, then turn under, pin and stitch a double hem along the length.

Kick Pleat
If there is no center seam, slit the lining to correspond with the pleat. Turn under a narrow double hem. Pin and stitch. Press in a fold at the top.

Trousers
Many linings can be secured under the garment hem, as here. This method works especially well on trousers, but can also be used for skirts.

Lining a Jacket

1 Finish the jacket, including hems. Assemble the lining, adding an extra 1 in (2.5 cm) to the center back. With wrong sides together, match darts and align the open seams to face each other along one underarm and side seam. Pin and baste the seam allowance on the garment to the seam on the lining. Stitch from the underarm to the bottom, then from the underarm to the cuff.

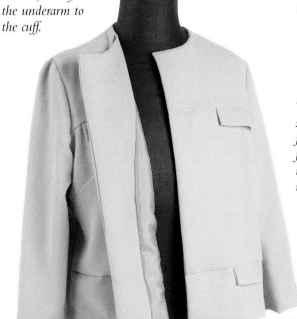

2 Pull the lining through to the wrong side of the garment and pin in place along the edges of the neck and facings. Be sure to allow enough slack as you work.

4 Turn under all the edges of the lining and slipstitch the lining to the jacket all around. The finished lined jacket is now ready for buttonholes to be worked (see page 78).

3 At the center back, match the darts on each side and pin a pleat to take up the excess fabric. Pin a corresponding pleat at the lower edge.

USEFUL TIP

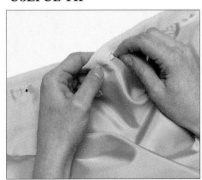

To add a lining to an unlined finished garment, turn under and pin the raw edge of the lining in place. Slipstitch neatly all along the edge, taking care not to sew through to the right side of the garment.

Alterations

DRESSMAKING PATTERNS CAN BE purchased in a variety of sizes; occasionally the standard measurements coincide with individual measurements, but often some alteration is needed to make a pattern that gives a perfect fit. To adjust a commercial pattern, begin by taking body measurements and examining the pattern for sizing (see page 24).

Generally, a cut is made in a pattern and a new piece is inserted to enlarge a measurement, or an overlap is created to reduce a measurement. Each pattern piece has strategic points where enlarging and reducing need to be done, and these are outlined on the following pages. Alterations can be made on a paper pattern, or one cut from inexpensive fabric.

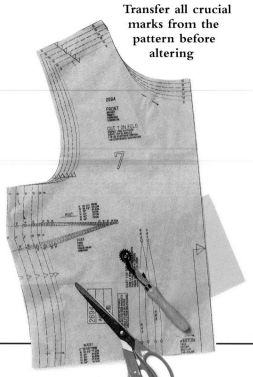

Transfer all crucial marks from the pattern before altering

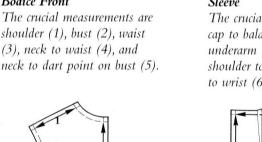

Bodice Front
The crucial measurements are shoulder (1), bust (2), waist (3), neck to waist (4), and neck to dart point on bust (5).

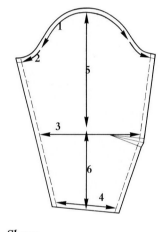

Sleeve
The crucial measurements are sleeve cap to balance marks (1), sleeve cap to underarm (2), elbow (3), wrist (4), shoulder to elbow (5), and elbow to wrist (6).

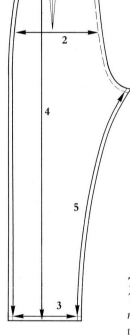

Trousers
The crucial measurements are waist (1), hips (2), hem (ankle) (3), waist to hem length (4), inside leg (5), side seam length (6), and crotch (7).

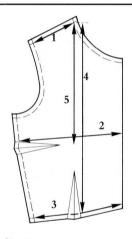

Bodice Back
The crucial measurements are shoulder (1), underarm to center back (2), waist (3), and neck to waist (4).

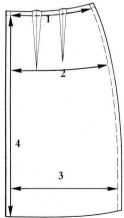

Skirt
The crucial measurements are waist (1), hips (2), hem (3), and waist to hem length (4).

Using Patterns and Paper

To reduce the size of a purchased pattern slightly, you can fold a crease in the pattern and secure it in place with pins or tape. The altered paper pattern can then be pinned to the garment fabric and cut out as usual.

To enlarge a paper pattern, particularly one that will be used only once, it is possible to add narrow pieces cut from strong paper. Pin or tape the paper strips carefully to vents cut into the pattern piece, as described in the examples below, before pinning to the fabric and cutting out. If you wish to reuse the pattern at a later date, it is best to cut each pattern piece from inexpensive cotton lining fabric and alter these before cutting out the garment (see pages 84–5), rather than cut into the original pattern.

Where to Measure

To achieve a perfect fit, you need to be aware of the places where patterns can be altered.

These diagrams include the measurements crucial to success. Always use a flexible tape measure to measure people and patterns, both paper and fabric ones.

TECHNIQUES	page
Basting	33
Marking	27
Understanding patterns	24

Taping Paper Vents
When enlarging a paper pattern, always use transparent tape to attach the paper so that any markings that appear on the pattern can be easily read.

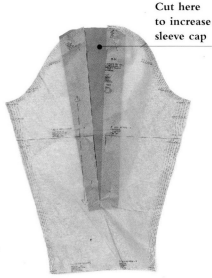

Cut here to increase sleeve cap

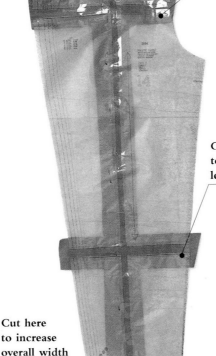

Cut here to increase crotch depth

Cut here to increase length

Cut here to increase overall width

Increasing Sleeve Cap Size
To make a sleeve cap larger, or to make a full gathered sleeve cap from a more tailored one, cut the pattern from the center balance mark on the sleeve cap, as shown. Pin or tape paper into the vent to the required width and into the full depth of the vent, easing the cut down until the pattern lies flat.

Increasing Width and Length
To make trousers or skirts longer, cut the pattern widthwise above the hem. To increase the crotch depth on trousers, cut across the hip line. To add width to trousers or skirts, cut the pattern into two pieces along the full length from the waist to the hem. Do not cut into a dart or any other marking at the waist. In each case, pin or tape paper into the vent to the required width.

USING A TOILE

Cutting a pattern from an inexpensive cotton fabric means that it can be used more than once. To make a toile, or fabric pattern, pin the commercial pattern to the fabric, then cut out and transfer all crucial markings, such as darts. Decide where you need to reduce or enlarge, using the examples shown here, then either cut into the fabric pattern and insert strips of fabric to the required width to enlarge, or fold over excess fabric and pin in place to reduce. Try the piece on to check the fit. Examine the original pattern again, transferring any remaining pattern markings, taking the alterations into account.

Reducing Skirt Fullness

1 *Cut from the hem to the hipline of the pattern. Do not cut through darts or other crucial markings. Overlap the cut edges until the required width is attained. Pin the overlapped edges in place.*

2 *The pinned piece can now be pinned to the garment fabric and cut out as usual. The overlapped edges can be basted together to secure them, if desired.*

Increasing Skirt Fullness

1 *To make a skirt fuller, cut the pattern piece as in step 1 of Reducing Skirt Fullness, above. Cut a strip of fabric wider than the required increase. Starting at the top of the cut vent, pin the strip in place along the two cut edges until the required width is reached.*

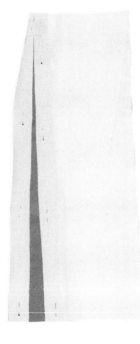

2 *The altered pattern piece is now ready to be pinned to the garment fabric and cut out. The pinned edges can be basted to secure them further.*

Increasing Crotch Depth

1 *To make the crotch deeper on a trouser pattern, cut from the center seam almost to the seamline on the side. Work above the curved area of the center seam and below any darts or other waistline markings. Pin in a strip of fabric wider than the required increase, as above, until the required depth is attained.*

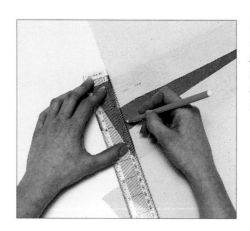

2 *Straighten the cutting line by marking, as shown. The marked cutting line can be trimmed away or cut off as you cut out the garment.*

Reducing Bodice Fullness

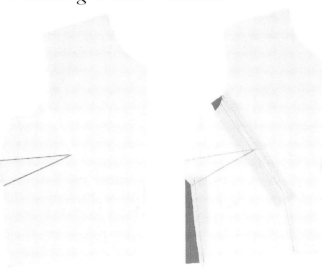

Altering the Front

Mark any darts or other crucial markings before cutting into the fabric pattern. Cut up from the waist of the bodice front piece, almost parallel to the center seam, then across on a diagonal line that ends above the bottom curve of the armhole and avoids the point of the dart, as shown left. Overlap the cut edges until the required reduction is made and the desired front measurement is reached. An extra strip of fabric may need to be added at the side seam to even up the edge, as shown right.

Altering the Back

Cut from the waistline, almost parallel to the center back seam, then at a sharper angle to finish near the middle of the shoulder seam, avoiding any crucial markings, as shown left. Overlap the cut edges until the required reduction is made and the desired back measurement is reached. Pin in place. If the overlap is very narrow, stitch it down to a backing strip of fabric to secure the alteration, as shown right. Add fabric to the side seam, if necessary, to straighten the cutting line.

Increasing Bodice Fullness

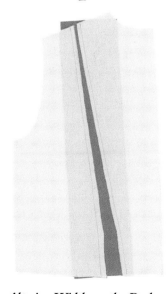

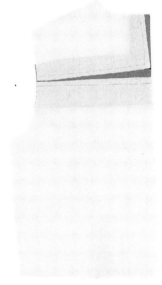

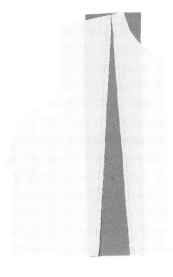

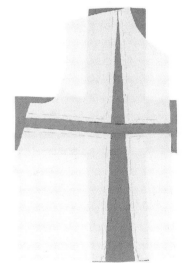

Altering Width on the Back

Cut from the waistline to the shoulder seam, as shown. Cut a strip of fabric wide enough to lie flat under the cut edges. Adjust to enlarge the pattern to the required measurement, then pin and stitch the strip in place.

Altering Length on the Back

Cut from the center back to finish between the shoulder and the underarm curve, as shown. Pin and stitch a strip of fabric to the required measurement, adding a vertical strip to straighten the center back cutting line, if necessary.

Altering Width on the Front

Cut from the waist to the shoulder seam, avoiding darts and other crucial markings. Cut a strip of fabric and pin it to the pattern, adjusting until the required measurement is reached. Stitch in position.

Altering Length and Width on the Front

Widen the pattern, as shown left, then cut it into two pieces between the armhole and the bustline dart. Pin in a fabric strip to the required measurement and stitch in place. Level all cutting lines.

Customizing

THE DRESSMAKING techniques in this book can be used, with a little imagination, to give old, outgrown or secondhand garments a new life and look. You will need to refer to the relevant entry in the Dressmaking chapter; for instance, if you are altering a shirt, look at the sections on sleeves, cuffs and collars on pages 54–61. Most of the ideas shown here can be applied to many different garments.

Customizing Dresses

Dresses can often be remodelled to extend their life. The skirt portion of the dress is usually easier to use than the top, but with careful planning you can use both.

Darts shape the waistline

Cutting Down a Dress
A dress can often be cut along the waistline and turned into a skirt. The double-buttoned skirt, above, has had darts added front and back to shape the waist (see page 50). A ribbon facing has been sewn along the top to finish the raw edges.

Finish armholes with bias binding

Easy-fit elastic waistband

Making a Skirt and Bolero
There was enough fullness in the waist of this dress to make an elasticized waistband on the skirt (see page 63). The bolero retains the neckline and button band of the dress top, but the sleeves have been removed. A coordinated ready-made bias binding was used to face the armholes and the bottom edge.

Lengthening and Shortening
Techniques for making dresses longer or shorter are particularly useful for children's clothes. The tucks in the pink and white gingham are worked along the line of the weave, and can be removed easily to make the dress longer (see page 51). The plain gathered ruffle lengthens the print dress to give a few more months of wear (see page 42). A row of matching bias binding (see page 44) has been added around the collar.

Tucks shorten the dress

A decorative ruffle lengthens the dress

Customizing Shirts and Blouses

Shirts and blouses are ideal candidates for customizing. Sleeves can be cut to a variety of lengths, or they can be eliminated altogether. Cuffs can be added to contrast or coordinate. Pockets can be removed, added or replaced. Necklines can be altered too; collars can be taken away or added, trimmed with lace or binding or cut down to a different shape.

● ● ● ● ● ● ● ● ● ● ●

TECHNIQUES	page
Alterations	82

A Mandarin collar is created from a tailored collar

Shirt-tail Effects

On this shirt, the shirt-tails have been cut off and new, reshaped, ones added. The stylish look is accentuated by the addition of cuffs on the sleeves and new buttons. Shirt-tails can also be stitched on straight-hemmed shirts to create extra length.

Summer Shirt Style

A simple plaid shirt has been made more suitable for the summer season. The sleeves have been removed and the armholes faced with bias binding (see page 54). The pointed collar was carefully taken out, and the stand portion restitched to make a Mandarin collar (see page 61). A discarded sleeve could have been made into another pocket.

Customizing Jackets

Plain jackets like these lend themselves well to customizing ideas, as seen by their new incarnations on the right. Bear in mind that garments made of natural fibers are easier to work on than synthetic ones, and are less likely to fray.

A decorative edge emphasizes the jacket shape

New pockets have been added in contrasting fabric

Decorative Edging

Here a patterned bias binding has been applied around the jacket's cuffs, collar and buttonhole band (see page 44) to transform a plain jacket into part of an ensemble.

Pockets and Cuffs

The pockets on this jacket have been removed and used as patterns for the striped replacements. A deep facing has been added to the cuffs, which are then turned back to reveal the decoration. New color-coordinated buttons complete the look.

HOME FURNISHINGS

Making your own home furnishings can be highly satisfying, but the sheer size of items like curtains or covers can also make it a daunting prospect. This chapter covers bedlinen including sheets, pillowcases, duvets and bedspreads; curtains and blinds, both lined and unlined; table linen; cushions of all types; and covers for sofas and chairs. Clear diagrams show you how to measure and there are lots of ideas for decorative touches.

Sheets

ALTHOUGH BED SHEETS are relatively inexpensive to buy ready-made, making your own can be rewarding, especially if you want a particular color to match your decor. Extra-wide sheeting fabric, sold in various colors and patterns, can be used to make pillowcases and duvet covers, too. Plain-colored bedlinen can be decorated in a variety of ways, and you can also use a ready-made flat sheet to make a fitted one by following the instructions below, provided you first cut off all the hems evenly.

Flat Sheet

Making a flat sheet is simplicity itself, provided the edges are absolutely level along the straight grain of the fabric. After levelling the edges, pin a double hem around all four sides. Baste the corners to secure them neatly, then machine-stitch all around.

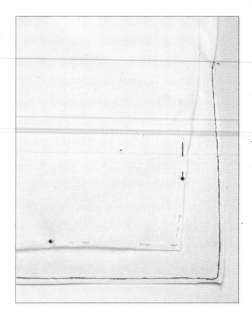

Fitted Sheet

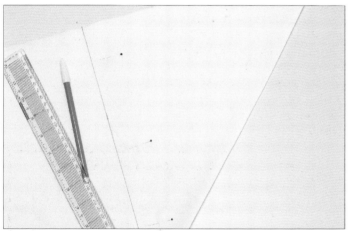

1 *Level all edges and fold each corner, as shown. Pin the fold and mark a 90-degree angle from the edge of the sheet to the fold. The marked line should measure the depth of the mattress plus 4 in (10 cm) allowance for underlap and seams.*

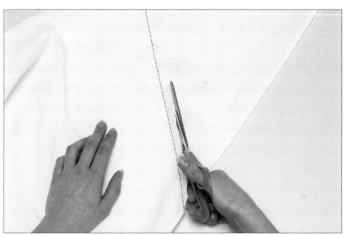

2 *Stitch along marked line. Trim the seam allowance to ¹/₂ in (1.25 cm). Press seam open and finish edges. To calculate the amount of elastic, multiply the length of the mattress by 2, plus the width of the mattress by 2, and subtract 10 in (25 cm) from the total. Cut ¹/₂ in (1.25 cm) wide elastic to this length.*

3 *Turn up a casing wide enough to thread through the elastic (see page 63). Pin in place and stitch all around, leaving a gap at one corner. Thread the elastic through and secure by overlapping the ends and stitching them together.*

4 *The finished sheet will fit neatly over the corners of the mattress. It is possible to use shorter lengths of elastic inserted securely at each corner only, leaving the long sides simply hemmed.*

Decorative Bordered Sheet

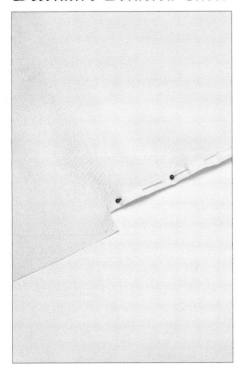

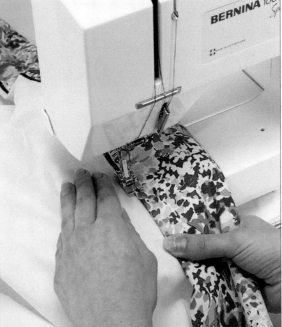

1 *Measure the desired depth of the border at the top end of the sheet and clip both side edges to mark. Turn under a double hem along the two sides and the bottom edges of the sheet and pin, as shown. Stitch to hem.*

2 *Cut the border fabric to the desired depth of the border and the width of the sheet, plus extra for seam allowances and hems. Join strips if necessary. With the wrong side of the sheet matching the right side of the border, pin and stitch the border to the top edge. Stitch the raw edges on each side. Turn the border to the right side of the sheet and press.*

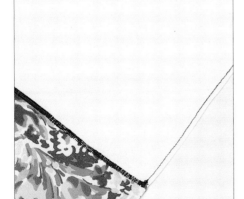

DECORATIVE BORDERS

A wealth of sewing techniques and ideas can be put to good use in decorative borders. Shown here, from the top: a piped corner, which is especially suitable for tailored pillowcases; a piped edge, which is then turned back to make a deep border; a border in a plain contrasting fabric with wide lace trim; insertion lace combined with a backing in a contrasting fabric; and broderie anglaise (eyelet) lace trim with a contrasting ribbon threaded through.

3 *Turn under the raw edge at the bottom of the border strip and pin in place. Topstitch to secure. A wide satin stitch has been used to create a decorative finish.*

4 *The decorative border can match a valance or duvet cover, or tie in with your room decor. Borders can be added to ready-made sheets if you wish.*

Pillowcases

ALTHOUGH MANY STYLES OF PILLOWCASE are inexpensive to buy, making your own is simple to do and allows you to match your pillows to other bedlinen and your bedroom decor. Pillowcases are first and foremost a protective covering for pillows. They can be plain and hidden beneath the bedspread, or they can be decorative statements that you will want to display on the top of the bed.

Top-opening Pillow Slip

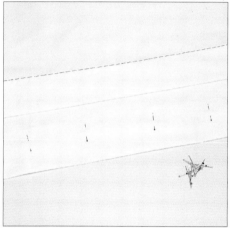 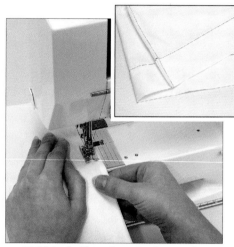 

1 Measure, mark and cut one piece of fabric measuring twice the length, plus hem allowances, of the pillow times the width of the pillow, plus seam allowances. Turn under a deep hem at each short end. Pin in place, and then stitch.

2 Fold in half to align the hemmed edges and pin the long edges together. To make a French seam, as shown, stitch with the wrong sides together, then turn out and stitch the seams with right sides together (see inset and page 37).

3 The pillow simply slides into the finished pillowcase, which can be decorated as desired (see Decorative Borders, page 91).

Back-opening Pillowcase

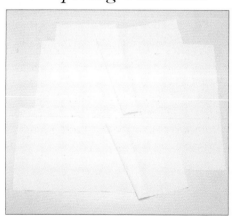 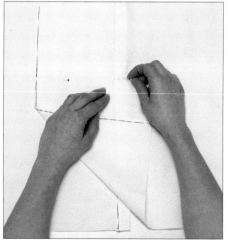 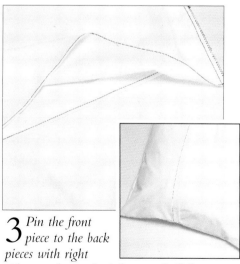

1 Measure, mark and cut three pieces. Cut the front piece to the size of the pillow plus seam allowances. The two back pieces meet in the middle and overlap to hold the pillow in place, and they should each be the same length and about three-quarters of the width of the front piece.

2 Turn under one long side of each back piece, and make a deep double hem in one and a narrow double hem in the other. Place the narrow-hemmed piece right side up and position the deep-hemmed piece right side up on top. Overlap the back pieces to the same size as the front.

3 Pin the front piece to the back pieces with right sides together and stitch around all four sides. Finish seam allowances. Inset: Turn right sides out and insert the pillow through the overlapped opening.

'Housewife' Pillowcase

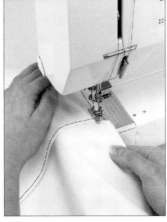

1 *Measure, mark and cut one piece of fabric measuring twice the length, plus hems and flap, of the pillow times the width of the pillow, plus seam allowances. Make one deep hem and one narrow hem on the short ends. With right sides together, fold back the narrow hem to make a flap.*

2 *Fold in half to align the hemmed edges. With wrong sides together, pin and stitch the long seams, as described in step 2 of the Top-opening Pillow Slip.*

3 *The finished pillowcase shows the flap inside the pillowcase, just visible here through the fabric. The flap holds the pillow securely in place.*

Ruffled Pillowcase

1 *Cut three pieces, as in step 1 of the Back-opening Pillowcase. Cut a ruffle piece to the desired width, plus seam allowances, and to twice the length of the four outside edges, plus allowances. Join strips as necessary. Make a double hem in one long edge and run a double row of gathering stitches in the other. Pull up the gathering and pin to the front piece with right sides together.*

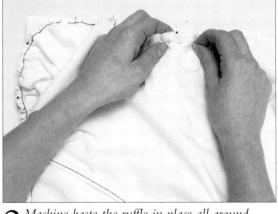

2 *Machine baste the ruffle in place all around. Make the back of the pillowcase as described in step 2 of the Back-opening Pillowcase. Baste the overlapped edges to secure them, then pin the back to the front with right sides together and enclosing the ruffle completely.*

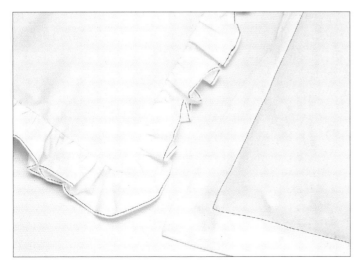

3 *Stitch around all four sides on top of the machine-basted seam. Remove basting in back opening, turn right sides out and insert the pillow, as shown left. The tailored version, shown right, is made by completing the back-opening pillowcase without a ruffle, and then stitching a wide border around all four edges. Remember to add the measurement for the border before cutting out pieces.*

Duvet Covers and Duvets

DUVETS AND THEIR COVERS can be expensive to buy, and both are straightforward to make. Duvet covers can be made from one fabric, embroidered or appliquéd, or reversible (as shown here for clarity). There are a variety of fasteners available, and some of these are decorative as well as easy to insert and practical to use. The two duvets shown here can be used separately or fastened together to make a cold-weather version.

Duvet Cover

1 *Measure, mark and cut two pieces of fabric to the length and width of the duvet, plus seam allowances and hems. Join pieces of fabric, if necessary. You could use two coordinated flat sheets if you wish, trimming off hems before you pin. Turn under, pin and stitch a deep hem on one short end of each piece.*

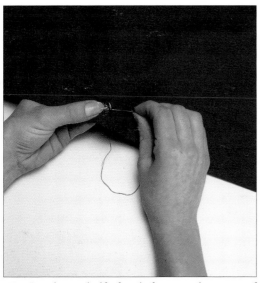

2 *Attach one half of each fastener along one of the hemmed edges. Space each fastener at equal distances along the edge. Large individual popper snaps have been used here.*

3 *Sew the second half of each fastener onto the other hemmed edge, carefully matching each pair as you work to make sure that the fasteners align properly.*

4 *With wrong sides together, attach the fasteners and pin the remaining three sides of the duvet cover together.*

5 *Stitch around all three sides of the cover, using a French seam (see page 37) for strength and neatness.*

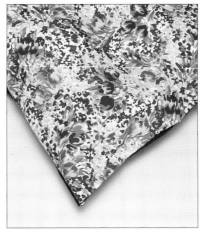

6 *The finished duvet cover is easy to remove for laundering. Other fasteners, such as buttons and buttonholes, or zippers or popper snap tape bought by the length, can be used (see pages 76–9).*

DUVET FASTENINGS

There are many ways of closing the end of a duvet cover. Coordinating ties (see page 133) and touch-and-close tape are just two easy and attractive options.

Making a Duvet

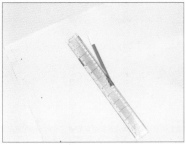

1 Measure, mark and cut two pieces from sturdy cotton fabric to the desired size of the duvet, plus seam allowances. Mark the channel stitching lines. Pin the two pieces with right sides facing.

2 Stitch securely around three sides, leaving a short end unstitched. Turn the duvet right side out through the short unstitched end.

3 Pin and stitch the marked channels, leaving 1 in (2.5 cm) or so at the top of each seam at the unstitched end.

4 Stuff each channel with batting (wadding) or other suitable filler. To stuff the channels of large duvets more easily, hang the open end of the duvet on a clothesline. Fold the open top edges to the inside and pin.

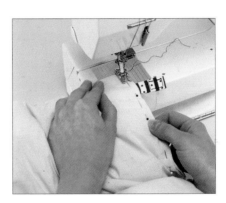

5 Machine-stitch the top edge to close, incorporating tabs (see Useful Tip) if desired.

Lightweight Duvet

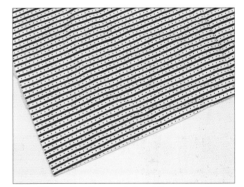

1 Measure, mark and cut two fabric pieces and one sheet of batting (wadding) to the desired size of the duvet, plus seam allowances. Place the fabric right sides together with the batting on top and pin.

2 Taking a seam allowance of 1/2 in (1 cm), stitch around three sides of the duvet, through all three layers and leaving one short end unstitched.

3 Turn the duvet right sides out. Measure and mark channels at equal distances to secure the batting (wadding) evenly. Pin and stitch the channels through all three layers.

4 Turn in the raw edges at the unstitched end and pin. Stitch to close, catching in tabs at each end if desired (see Useful Tip). Use the tabs to join two lighter-weight duvets together to make a heavy-duty duvet, as shown here.

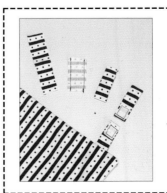

USEFUL TIP

To make tabs, cut strips measuring 1 x 3 in (2.5 x 7.5 cm). Fold each in half, right sides together, and stitch the two long sides. Then turn right sides out and press. Add fasteners to the folded ends. Catch the raw end of each tab into the seam at the duvet corners.

Bedspreads

BEDS ARE NATURAL FOCAL POINTS and the cover that you choose can set the tone for the entire bedroom. Simple throws can be used as bedspreads, as well as gracing sofas or chairs – not necessarily in the bedroom. Plain hemmed bedspreads and throws are straightforward to make and can be embellished with trims and made in a variety of styles. Fitted bedspreads and valances offer a more traditional approach to bed furnishings; they are a little more complicated to make and accurate measuring is necessary.

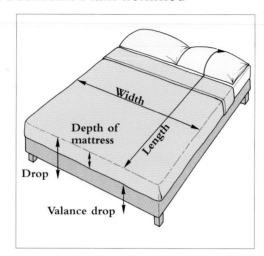

Width

Depth of mattress

Drop

Length

Valance drop

Measuring Bedspreads
Always add on 1/2 in (1.25 cm) for every seam allowance and 1 in (2.5 cm) for each hem. The deck piece will be the same for bedspreads or valances, and should measure the length and width of the mattress. For a bedspread skirt, measure the drop to the floor from the top of the mattress. For a valance skirt, measure the drop to the floor from just under the mattress.

The length for the skirt will vary. Add the measurement of the two long and one short sides of the bed. If gathered, multiply by 2 1/2–3; if tailored, add a yard (meter) for the two pleats.

Curved Throw

1 *Pin the binding along the edge of levelled fabric (see page 44). To join lengths of binding, fold the ends under by 1/2 in (1 cm), place against each other and pin in place.*

2 *Pin and baste the binding around the corner curves, keep the binding slack. Machine-stitch around the throw, keeping the edges of binding and fabric level.*

3 *Fold the binding to the wrong side to cover the raw edge. Working with the right side up, pin the binding beside the stitched edge, as shown.*

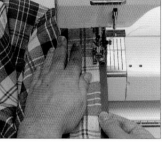

4 *Machine-stitch the binding in position. Ease the binding carefully around the curved corners.*

Curved hem

Plain hem

Plain Throw

1 *Level the edges of the fabric, making sure that all four corners are perfectly square. Turn under and pin a double hem all around. Do not pin the corners.*

2 *Miter each corner carefully (see page 41) and baste it in place. Use as small stitches as possible so that the corners are held securely.*

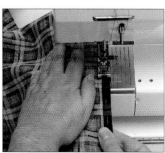

3 *Working from the wrong side, machine-stitch the hem. At the corners, leave the needle in the fabric and turn at a right angle to give a neat finish.*

Reversible throw

Reversible Throw

 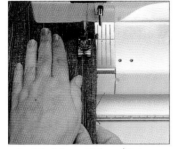 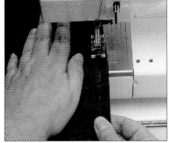

1 *A reversible throw is made from two fabrics back to back. Level the edges of both. Lay the pieces together, right side to right side.*

2 *Machine-stitch a ½ in (1.5 cm) seam all around, leaving a 10 in (25 cm) gap in the center of one side. Turn the throw right sides out through the gap.*

3 *Fold the gap in neatly and press all the edges. Topstitch ½ in (1.5 cm) in from the edge to strengthen and finish the throw.*

Hand Fringing

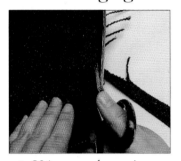  

Hand fringing

1 *Using very sharp scissors, trim each edge level. Follow the weave on each side as closely as possible.*

2 *Fray each edge to the desired depth, carefully using a pin to tease out the individual threads.*

3 *Zigzag around all edges with a medium-size stitch, working as close to the fringe as possible.*

Ready-made Fringing

Ready-made fringing

 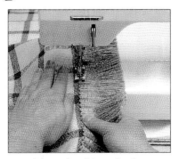 

1 *Level the edges of the fabric and pin the fringe so that it overlaps the fabric edge slightly. With the fringe facing up, stitch along the trim's edge.*

2 *Turn the fringe back to cover the raw edge of the fabric and pin it in place. Pay particular attention to corners, basting them if necessary.*

3 *Machine-stitch the top edge of the fringe along all sides to finish. Use the fringe with the trim showing on the right side, or on the wrong side, as you prefer.*

FITTED BEDSPREADS

Fitted bedspreads and valances are made in a similar way. A bedspread has a 'skirt' piece that drops to the floor and is attached to a 'deck' piece, which covers the mattress, whereas a valance fits under the mattress. A valance stays in place most of the time, whereas a fitted spread covers the entire bed and will probably be laundered more often. Furnishing-weight fabrics are appropriate for tailored spreads, but flounced and ruffled spreads can be made from fabrics such as lighter cottons and polyester cottons. Use the guidelines shown on page 96 to measure for bedspreads and valances.

Flounced Bedspread

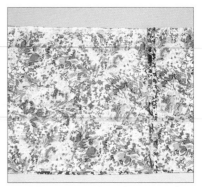

1 *Measure, mark and cut out the deck piece, adding an extra 2 in (5 cm) to the length (see step 4). Turn under and stitch a deep double hem along the top edge.*

2 *Measure, mark and cut out the skirt piece, joining short ends as necessary to make up the required length. Press and finish the short seams. Hem one long edge and both short free ends.*

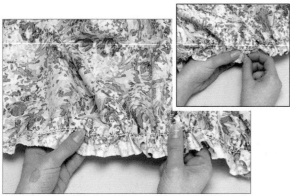

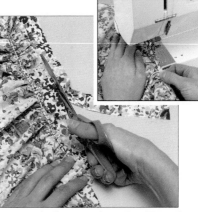

3 *Measure and cut a length of cord or string the same length as the skirt piece. Pin it along the long raw edge of the skirt, about 1¹/2 in (4 cm) in. Using a wide zigzag stitch, sew the cord in place. Do not catch the cord in the stitching. Pull up the cord to gather. Inset: Pin the skirt piece to the deck piece around the three unhemmed sides, adjusting gathers evenly.*

4 *Stitch the pieces together. Trim the top of the skirt piece to about ¹/2 in (1.5 cm) and the raw edge of the deck to 1¹/2 in (4 cm). Inset: Fold over and pin the raw edge of the deck to enclose the top of the skirt, then stitch.*

5 *The finished bedspread gives a soft, feminine look to a bedroom.*

Headed Ruffle Bedspread

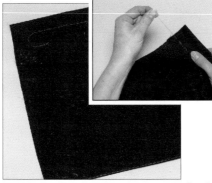

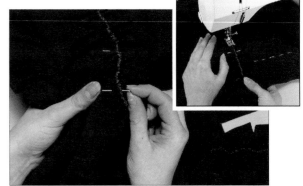

1 *Measure and cut out deck, adding 2 in (5 cm) all around. Baste all sides 2 in (5 cm) from edge to mark mattress size. Make a double hem in the top edge along basted line.*

2 *Make the skirt piece as in step 2 of the Flounced Bedspread. Fold over the top of the skirt piece once and make a casing through both layers 1¹/2 in (4 cm) deep using two rows of gathering stitch. Inset: Pull up carefully to gather.*

3 *Pin the wrong side of the gathered skirt piece to the right side of the deck piece, following the basted line and positioning the short ends of the skirt 2 in (5 cm) in from the top of the deck. Inset: Stitch the skirt piece in place. Remove the gathering threads.*

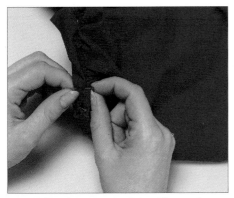

4 *Following step 4 of the Flounced Bedspread, trim the raw edges of the deck and skirt. Fold and pin the edge of the deck over to enclose the raw edge of the skirt, then stitch.*

5 *The inside of the seam joining the skirt to the deck is now neat. Remove the basting stitches on the deck piece.*

6 *The finished bedspread is eyecatching and would be an attractive feature in most bedrooms.*

Tailored Bedspread

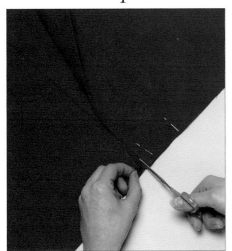

1 *Make the deck piece and skirt following steps 1 and 2 of the Flounced Bedspread. Mark the two corner pleats in the skirt piece and press the folds in place. Pin in position and snip 1/2 in (1.5 cm) down the center of each pleat. Baste each pleat closed to secure.*

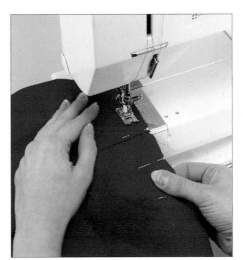

2 *With right sides together, pin the skirt piece to the unfinished short end of the deck. Stitch in place along the short edge only, beginning and ending in the center of a pleat.*

3 *Pin and stitch one long side and then the other. Inset: Before beginning stitching, fold back each pleat as shown. Backstitch at corner pleats to secure and finish the edges.*

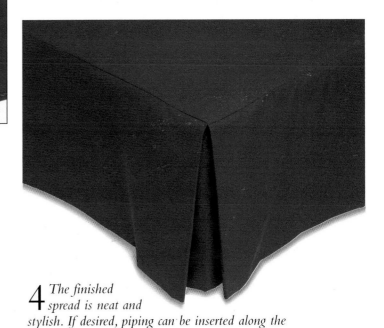

4 *The finished spread is neat and stylish. If desired, piping can be inserted along the seam that joins the skirt to the deck (see page 46).*

Simple Quilting

QUILTING GENERALLY INVOLVES stitching together three layers, consisting of a sheet of batting (wadding) sandwiched between a top fabric and a backing fabric. A length of fabric can be quilted before cutting out pieces, and jackets, waistcoats and many home accessories, such as placemats and cushion covers, can be made this way. Specialist equipment is not needed for simple quilting, but you may like to invest in such items as quilting threads, frames and thimbles as your interest develops.

Creative Effects
Machine quilting can be used to create many different designs. A twin needle is used on the top sample, and gold machine embroidery thread is stitched in a geometric pattern on the bottom piece.

Machine Quilting

1 *Mark the design on right side of the top piece of fabric with a water-soluble pen or chalk. Small pieces can be marked lightly, but larger pieces need stronger markings to withstand more handling.*

2 *Baste together the fabric to be quilted, the batting (wadding) and the backing fabric so all layers are secure. Start from the middle of the piece and work out to the edge in each direction.*

3 *Working from the right side, machine-stitch along the marked lines. Use a fairly long stitch and follow the markings carefully. Trim the edges of all layers, if necessary.*

Machine-quilted Pieces
Even simple repetitive designs, such as the ones here, look effective. Be sure to baste carefully; if the layers move about, the tautness between the rows may be lost and the backing may pucker.

USEFUL TIP

There is a vast selection of preprinted panels available, which can be quilted by hand or machine and then made into quilts, bags, cushions and other items. They are usually sold by the panel, or strip of panels, or by the length, and many come with coordinating background fabric. The amount of quilting you add is up to you. The panel shown here uses both hand and machine quilting, including some zigzag rows to fill in such areas as the butterfly's body.

Hand Quilting

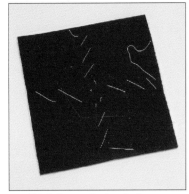

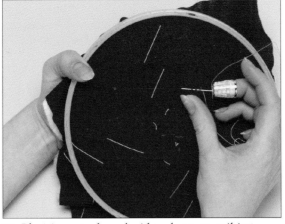

1 *Lightly mark the design on the top piece of fabric and baste all layers together, as for steps 1 and 2 of machine quilting. Larger pieces may need many rows of basting, radiating out from the center.*

2 *Place in a sturdy embroidery hoop or quilting frame. Use an 18-in (45-cm) length of quilting thread in a 'between' needle and tie a knot in one end. Pull the knot through the backing fabric so it is embedded in the batting (wadding). Work small, even running stitches along marked lines, through all layers.*

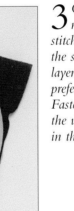

3 *Continue quilting around the marked design, keeping the stitches even. Aim to make stitches the same size on the top and bottom layers; big but even stitches are preferable to small irregular ones. Fasten off by knotting near the end of the work and again hiding the knot in the batting (wadding).*

Sashing a Quilt

1 *Quilted squares can be joined together with narrow strips, called sashing, to make a larger piece. To do this, trim all edges of each square evenly and cut strips of sashing to the desired width. Here the central rectangle has been sashed first, then the sashed squares are joined to it.*

2 *The resulting piece is a sampler of hand- and machine-quilted techniques. Adding a layer of batting (wadding), a backing for the entire piece and a binding (see page 44) would create a small quilt suitable as a throw or wall hanging.*

Hand-quilted Pieces
Hand quilting can be used to make designs of stark simplicity or startling complexity. Fabrics made from natural fibers, such as cotton or silk, are more satisfying to work on than blended or synthetic fabrics.

Curtains

THE STYLE, POSITION AND SHAPE of a window all play an important part in decisions about curtains. Window treatments can often transform a room. Small windows can be made to look larger; adjoining windows of different sizes can be unified by clever curtaining. Sheer curtains can provide privacy or mask an indifferent view while still allowing light to filter in. Making your own window coverings gives unlimited flexibility in coordinating decorating schemes, although curtain-making does require patience, accurate measuring and sufficient space to work.

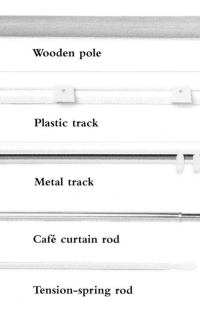

Wooden pole

Plastic track

Metal track

Café curtain rod

Tension-spring rod

Sheer spring wire

Curtain Hardware
The variety of poles, rods and tracks available can be confusing. The style of the room, the size and weight of the curtains and the preferred method of opening and closing the curtains must be considered when choosing hardware.

Measuring Windows

If possible, mount the curtain hardware before you measure a window. This will make it much easier to find the exact position of the top of the pole or track. Work out the length and width measurements of the finished curtain by using the diagram on the right as a guide.

To calculate the amount of fabric required, you will need to allow extra fabric for hems, headings and curtain fullness. To the finished window length, add 12–16 in (30–40 cm) for hems, plus twice the depth of the heading. Add one pattern repeat if applicable. Full curtains look best, so allow 2 to 2½ times the finished width for medium- or heavyweight fabrics; for sheer and lightweight fabrics, multiply the width by 2 to 3. The following example may help you work out your individual requirements.

For a mediumweight fabric, where the finished length is 75 in (1.9 m), the finished width is 48 in (1.2 m), and the heading is 4 in (10 cm):

Length		
	75 in	(1.9 m)
headings	8 in	(0.20 m)
hems	14 in	(0.35 m)
pattern repeat	6 in	(0.15 m)
Total length required	103 in	**(2.6 m)**
Width	48 in	(1.2 m)
multiplied by 2½		
Total width required	120 in	**(3 m)**

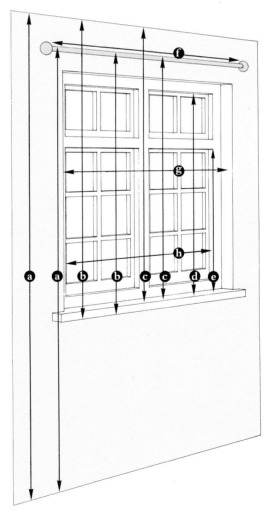

Length: vertical measurements

a ceiling or top of pole to floor

b ceiling or top of pole to bottom of window frame

c ceiling or top of pole to sill

d top of glazed area to sill

e sash to sill

Width: horizontal measurements

f ends of pole, track or rod

g outside edge of frame to opposite edge

h inside edge of frame to opposite edge

Sheer Curtains

Sheer curtains are not only very useful, they can also be extremely beautiful. The choice of fabrics available, some patterned with antique-style designs, is huge, and a well-chosen set of sheers can give definition to a room without costing the earth. Hung on a spring wire, or on a wooden pole as café curtains, sheers can screen a room from the outside without cutting out the view; very full draped swags of sheer fabric can give elegance to any room.

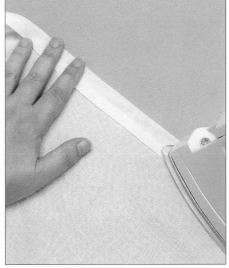

1 *Measure and cut out a length of fabric for the curtain. After levelling all the edges, stitch a double hem in each side edge. Make a casing for the curtain rod or pole by pressing a double fold in the top that is twice as wide as the rod or pole.*

● ● ● ● ● ● ● ● ● ● ● ● ● ●

TECHNIQUES	page
Basting	33
Hems	64
Marking	27
Pressing	40
Stitches	32

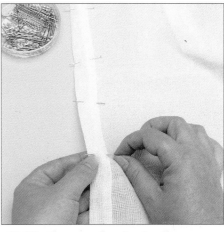

2 *Pin the pressed casing in place. Position the pins across the stitching line, as shown, so that you can stitch over them.*

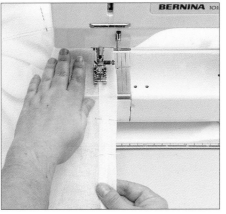

3 *Machine-stitch the casing along the inside edge of the fold, removing the pins as you work. Pin and stitch a double hem, 2 in (5 cm) deep, along the bottom edge.*

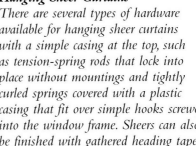

MEASURING FRENCH WINDOWS

French windows are fully glazed external doors. Outward-opening French windows can be measured and curtained in the same way as tall casement windows. If the doors open in, poles and tracks must be positioned so they allow the curtain to be pulled clear of the door when it is open.

MEASURING BAY WINDOWS

Separate curtains can be hung on individual tracks for each part of a bay window, but a long double run opening on each side is a more effective method. A track shaped to the window is needed, and can be ordered from a specialist supplier.

Hanging Sheer Curtains

There are several types of hardware available for hanging sheer curtains with a simple casing at the top, such as tension-spring rods that lock into place without mountings and tightly curled springs covered with a plastic casing that fit over simple hooks screwed into the window frame. Sheers can also be finished with gathered heading tape and hung with hooks (see page 106).

CAFE CURTAINS

Traditionally, café curtains hang across the lower section of a window on wooden or metal poles, though they can also hang from the top of a window. They allow light into the room but provide privacy and obscure the view. Café curtains can be made from virtually any fabric and can be headed with tabs and loops, as shown here, or with any of the more simple headings on pages 106-9.

Tabbed Café Curtains

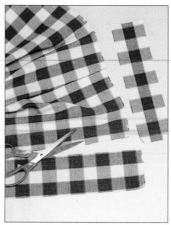

1 *Measure and cut out the main curtain piece, a wide facing strip for the heading and the required number of strips for the tabs.*

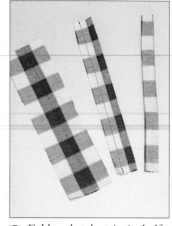

2 *Fold each tab strip in half lengthwise, wrong sides together, and stitch. Turn right side out and press with the seam centered on the back of the tab. Repeat for all the tabs. Here the tab is the same width as the dark blue stripe.*

3 *Zigzag raw edges of curtain pieces and one edge of facing strip. Fold over each tab with seam sides together and pin them at regular intervals between curtain and facing strip, right sides together with raw edges aligned.*

4 *Stitch the pinned seam, catching in both ends of each tab as you work. Stitch the short ends of the facing and clip the corners. The side edge seen here is a selvedge, so it was not zigzagged.*

5 *Turn right sides out so the facing lies on the wrong side of the curtain and press, turning under a narrow hem on the curtain sides. Topstitch all along the top edge and down each side.*

6 *Try the curtain on the pole and measure and mark the hem. Pin a single hem in place and stitch along the zigzagged edge, matching the pattern.*

7 *The finished café curtain simply slips over the ends of a curtain pole. The tabs are aligned to match the check in the fabric and easily slide along the pole to open or close the curtain.*

TIED CAFE CURTAINS

This variation of a tabbed café curtain uses bias binding to finish all four edges and make the ties (see page 44). The ties could be made from ribbon or any fabric, matching or contrasting, and tied in a bow, as shown, or knotted.

Scalloped Café Curtains

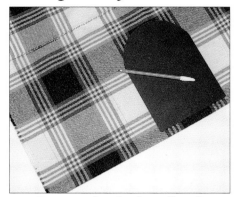

1 Cut a template for the scallops from cardboard. Measure and cut the curtain pieces and zigzag the top raw edge. Fold over the top zigzagged edge so right sides are together and mark the scallops at regular intervals.

2 Pin each scallop in place in the middle section, which is the area to be cut away. Pin through all the layers of fabric. Here the pattern of the fabric has been used to help space the loops evenly.

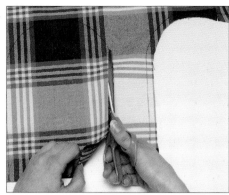

3 Stitch each scallop along the marked lines. Trim inside the stitched lines 3/8 in (1 cm) from the stitching. Clip the curves along each scallop and clip off corners. Do not cut through the stitching.

4 Turn the facing right side out and press. Fold each tab to the back and pin and stitch it in place along its top edge. This seam will appear as topstitching on the right side of the curtain. Make sure all the tabs are level. Turn under and hem the side edges as for step 5 of the tabbed café curtains.

5 Try the curtain on the pole. Measure, mark and stitch the bottom hem, as for step 6 of the tabbed café curtains. The last tab on each end is only half the width of the others.

Scalloped Curtains with Rings

The scallop technique lends itself to all sorts of effects. Here the scallop has been cut as a triangle and faced. The points have been folded to the front of the curtain and secured with buttons.

1 Measure and mark the fabric as in step 1 of the Scalloped Café Curtains but make shallower scallops. Stitch and trim as in steps 2 and 3.

2 Turn the scallops right side out and press. Hem the sides as in step 5 of the Tabbed Café Curtains. Attach clip-on rings on the center top of each tab.

3 Slide the rings over the pole. Measure, mark and stitch the bottom hem to finish the curtain as described in step 6 of the Tabbed Café Curtains.

CURTAIN HEADINGS

A wide choice of curtain heading tapes is available, ranging from simple gathered headings to highly formal pinch and pencil-pleated ones. Some consist of a heavy woven tape with cords laced through at intervals; others have pockets woven in, into which special hooks are inserted at regular intervals to make the pleats. All have woven guidelines that mark the stitching lines and make it simple to keep the seams straight. The tape needs to be as long as the full width of the curtain fabric, plus a generous allowance for turning under the ends.

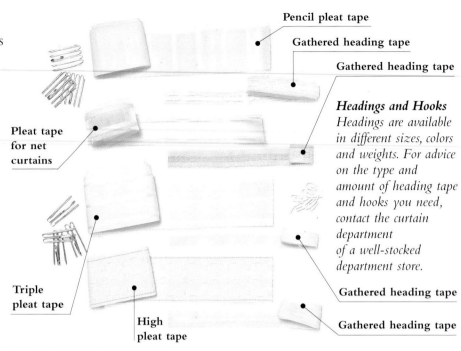

Pencil pleat tape

Gathered heading tape

Gathered heading tape

Pleat tape for net curtains

Headings and Hooks
Headings are available in different sizes, colors and weights. For advice on the type and amount of heading tape and hooks you need, contact the curtain department of a well-stocked department store.

Triple pleat tape

High pleat tape

Gathered heading tape

Gathered heading tape

Simple Gathered Heading

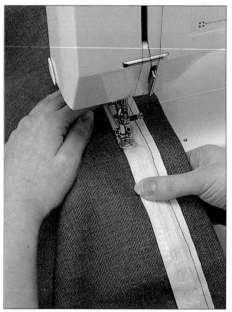

1 To make an unlined gathered curtain, measure, mark and cut the curtain pieces. Turn under, pin and hem the side edges of each piece, then finish the top raw edge. Turn back and pin a 2-in (5-cm) single fold at the top. Lay the heading tape, cord side up, along the finished raw edge and pin.

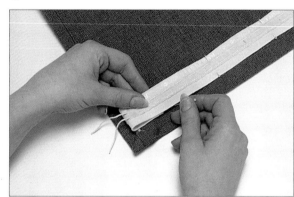

2 Turn under a partial miter (see page 41) at the side edge of the curtain to reduce bulk. Cut the tape, fold the end under and pin in place. Loosen the ends of the cords, but do not pull them up.

3 Stitch the tape in place along both long edges, following the woven guidelines marked on the heading tape to help keep the seams straight.

4 Hem the bottom of each curtain piece, measuring carefully to make sure that the desired finished length is reached. If you wish, enclose weights in the hem (see Useful Tip, opposite).

5 Knot the cords together at each end and pull the gathers. Work first from one end and then the other to meet in the middle.

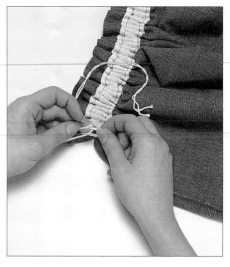

6 Tie the ends of the cords at each side edge in a slip knot so the heading is easy to loosen when removing the curtain for laundering.

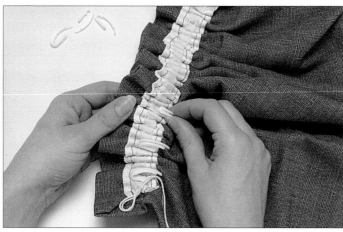

7 Insert the appropriate hooks to fit the curtain track. Space the hooks at regular intervals and even up the gathers as you work.

8 The finished curtain hangs in neat, simple folds from the gathered heading. Plain heading tape such as this is ideal for lightweight and medium-weight fabrics where a simple, uncluttered window dressing is required.

USEFUL TIP

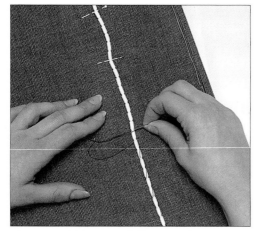

Curtain weights are available as metal squares or discs that are sewn into the hem like buttons or as strings purchased by length, as shown here.

To attach, pin the string in place along the fold of the hem and slipstitch it in place (see page 33). Catch a few threads of curtain fabric in the needle, then insert the needle through a space between the weights. Keep the stitches even and try to work into the turned-under side of the fold so that they are invisible when the curtain is hung. To finish, turn up the hem and stitch in place.

Double Pleat Heading

This tape pulls up to make a double pleat, which has been embellished with handmade embroidered buttons. There are also tapes available into which special pronged metal hooks are is inserted at regular intervals to create the pleats.

Back View
Make the curtains and apply the tape as shown on pages 106–7. Pull up the cords to form the pleats. Remember to knot the ends of the cords together before you pull. If the cord slips out of the heading, it cannot be re-strung.

Front View
A button has been stitched to the bottom of each pleat to add a decorative detail and hold the pleat in place. The buttons are self-covered in a fabric that coordinates with the curtain fabric, and they have been embroidered with four straight stitches to form a star (see inset).

Pencil Pleat Heading

Pencil pleats are simple unpressed folds that are evenly spaced and of equal depth. They give generous fullness and handsome body to curtains, hang beautifully and are suitable for most windows and styles of curtain track or pole.

Back View
The heading tape is applied in the same way as the simple gathered heading on pages 106–7. Be sure to tie all three cords together at each end before starting to pull up the pleats.

Front View
From the front, pencil-pleated curtains have a look that is unmatched by any other type of heading. They need fullness of 2 1/2 to 3 times the width of the window to be covered, depending on the weight of the fabric used.

Smocked Heading

This tape is designed to pull up into a neat line of smocking, which looks charming with most lightweight and medium-weight fabrics and is particularly effective in solid colors. It can be used to make pretty and unusual curtain valances, and gives a feminine touch to sheer curtains. A fullness of 2½ times the width of the curtains is required.

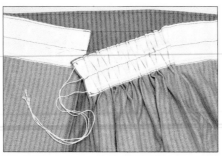

Back View
Apply this tape in a similar way to the simple gathered heading on pages 106–7, but note that there are three parallel lines of stitching, not just two. Be careful not to stitch over the cord when working the center line.

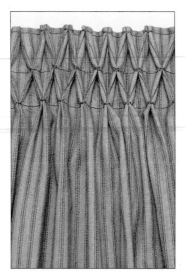

Front View
The tape automatically creates a smocked edge when the cords are pulled. The center and bottom points have been decoratively stitched with coordinating embroidery thread to enhance the smocked effect.

Triple Pleat Heading

The elegance of triple pleats, which fan out at the top, makes this heading a firm favorite, and most tapes have a choice of pockets for the hooks so the curtain can be hung below a decorative wooden pole or used to hide a track.

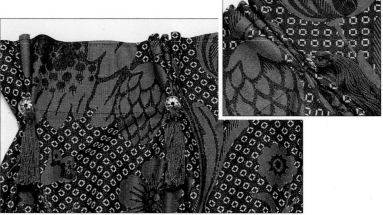

Back View
Triple-pleat tape is very wide and applied as described on pages 106–7. Always remember to tie each end of the cords before pulling up the pleats.

Front View
These pleats lend themselves to embellishment, especially as some manufacturers recommend making a small stitch at the bottom of each pleat to secure it. Inset: small tassels made by hand from embroidery thread (see page 117) have been threaded through a button before being stitched on each pleat.

Cartridge Pleat Heading

Cartridge pleats are similar to pencil pleats in appearance and construction, but are widely spaced and somewhat cylindrical. They require a little less fabric than pencil pleats – twice the width of the window – but are no less elegant. Most tapes are designed to hang below a curtain pole, but by moving the hooks to a different level, the tape can hide an ordinary track.

Back View
Cartridge-pleat tape is applied to a curtain in the same way as the gathered heading on page 106–7, with a seam stitched along the guidelines top and bottom.

Front View
Cartridge pleats are one of the most elegant of curtain headings and work particularly well on medium-weight and heavyweight fabrics. They are suitable for virtually any fabric design, and because of their depth, they work effectively with vertical patterns.

CURTAIN LININGS

Backing a curtain with a lining fabric is advisable, except for sheer curtains and those made from extremely lightweight fabrics. Linings give body, drape and shape to most curtains, and they help protect the curtain fabric from sunlight, which can damage fibers and cause discoloration. Special heavyweight linings can obscure or block light, and can help to insulate the room when the curtains are closed.

Perhaps the most difficult aspect of lining curtains is finding adequate work space, since it is necessary to lay the curtain flat in order to work on it. A large dining room table or a cleared floor space, preferably an uncarpeted one, can be used.

Hand-finished Lining

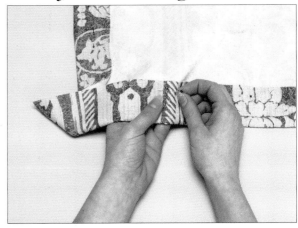

1 *Cut out the curtain, joining sections to make up the required width if necessary. Turn up and pin the side hems. Miter the corners (see page 41) and pin the bottom hem in place.*

2 *Herringbone-stitch (see page 33) the hem in place along the bottom and around the sides, removing pins as you work.*

3 *Cut out the lining to the same size as the curtains, but subtracting the hems. Stitch sections together as necessary to make up the required size. Turn under and machine-stitch the bottom and sides of the lining to hem. Mark guidelines on the wrong side of the lining to match the seams in the curtain.*

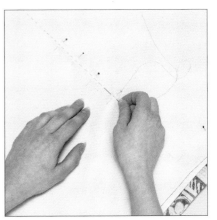

4 *Place the curtain and lining with wrong sides together. Match curtain seams to lining guidelines, smoothing outward, and pin. Baste along the guidelines. Here the right side of the lining has been marked for clarity.*

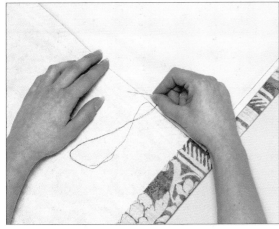

5 *Remove pins. Fold back the lining along the basted guideline and slipstitch the lining to the curtain (see page 33). On wide curtains with more than one seam, pin, baste and slipstitch one guideline at a time before moving on to the next.*

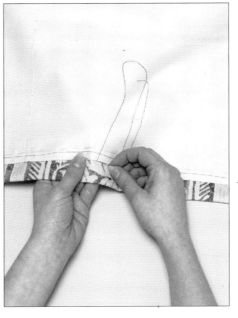

6 *Baste the lining in position along the sides and bottom of the curtain, then catchstitch it to the curtain hem. Finally, follow the instructions on pages 106–9 to insert a heading, treating the lining and the main fabric as one piece when turning under the top edge. If you are worried about shrinkage on either fabric, wash to preshrink before making up, or find an alternative fabric.*

Tube Lining

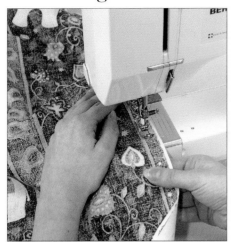

1 Measure and cut out the curtain and lining pieces. The lining should be about 8 in (20 cm) narrower than the curtain, but both should be the same length. With right sides together, stitch the lining and main fabric together at the side seams, stopping 6 in (15 cm) from the bottom.

2 Measure each side to turn back the edges of the main fabric evenly. The lining should be centered on the curtain. Here the stripe in the pattern has been used as a guide to the measurement of the side hems. Turn right sides out and press.

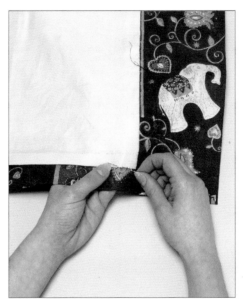

3 Establish the desired length of the curtain and pin the bottom edge of the main fabric in place, repeating for the lining. Machine-stitch the lining to hem, then miter the corners of the main curtain fabric and hem by hand.

4 Slipstitch the unsewn side edges of the lining to the curtain, catching in the bottom corner neatly. Insert the heading (see pages 106–9), measuring carefully to achieve the necessary length on the finished curtain and treating the lined curtain as one piece.

Loose Lining

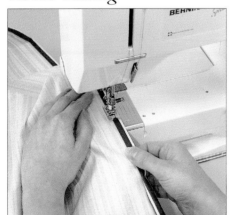

1 Cut the lining to the size of the curtain, but subtract the measurement for the side hems. Turn under and hem both sides of the lining.

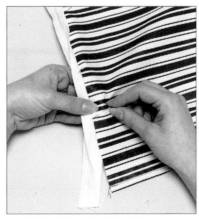

2 Use a length of heading tape to enclose the top raw edge of the lining, pinning it in place as shown. Pull the ends of the cords clear and fold under the short ends of the tape. Baste and stitch in place through all of the layers.

3 Insert hooks into the lining tape, then mount the lining onto the finished curtain. Hem the lining to the desired length. Pull up the lining cords as necessary when the curtain heading is pulled up. The lining can be easily removed for cleaning or during the warmer summer months.

Curtain Valances

A CURTAIN VALANCE, ALSO CALLED A PELMET, is practical and decorative. Curtain valances can stop light filtering through the top of curtains or help to keep a room warm and can provide a stylish heading for two or more windows.

Special valance tracks are available, but ordinary curtain tracks can be used. Flat or boxed valances can be made from plywood or fiberboard. A boxed valance is enclosed on the top and at both ends; enlist the help of a carpenter to make one to your specifications. Valances need to measure the width of the window plus enough allowance at each end to conceal the curtain hardware without interfering with the opening and closing mechanism. The depth of the valance depends on the style, length and fullness of the curtains.

Flat Valance

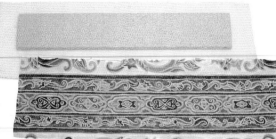

1 *Measure and cut the backing board, batting (wadding) and fabric. The fabric and batting should wrap around the board to cover the top and bottom edges and the ends easily.*

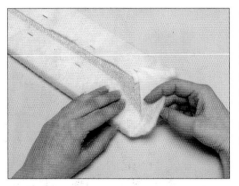

2 *Staple, glue or nail the batting on the back of the board. Secure the long edges first, then trim the corners to reduce bulk. Turn the ends to the back to cover the short edges.*

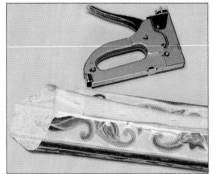

3 *Stretch the fabric across the board and staple, glue or nail it in place, as for the batting. Trim the corners to reduce bulk and turn them neatly to the back to conceal edges.*

4 *The finished valance is ready to be mounted on the window. This type of valance is most useful on windows set in an alcove or recess where there is no room for a more bulky box valance. It can be mounted on brackets that are hidden from front and side views.*

Box Valance

1 *Cover the box base with batting (wadding) as in step 3 of the Flat Valance, or cut separate pieces and glue in place. Do not pad the edges that will rest against the wall.*

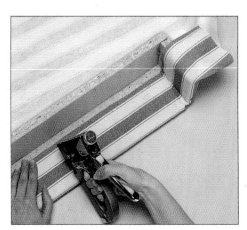

2 *Cut the fabric large enough to cover the box completely. Staple, glue or nail it in place along the long edges inside the box, then fold the corners neatly and secure them in place.*

3 *A box valance can be used with curtains, or with blinds as shown here. The ends are visible, so it is important to finish them neatly. The top of the valance can rest on flat brackets mounted above the window frame.*

Box-pleated Valance

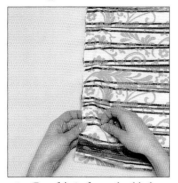

2 Cut a strip of fabric wide enough to bind the top edge (see page 44). With right sides together, pin and stitch along the long edge. Turn the strip to the back, turn the raw edge under and stitch along the long and short ends.

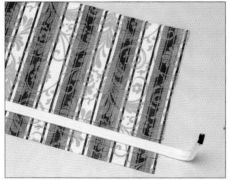

1 Cut fabric for a doubled box-pleated strip (see page 42) to cover the front and ends of a box valance. Fold short ends to the wrong side and fold the strip in half lengthwise. Press and pin pleats, then stitch across the top.

3 Use the pleated valance to cover a board box valance. The strip of binding fabric at the top folds neatly over the top edge of the valance and can be stapled in place. Turn the corners carefully, folding the binding before stapling.

Gathered Valance

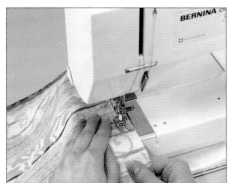

1 Measure and cut one piece of fabric twice the depth of the desired valance, plus seams and at least the same width as the curtains, plus seams. Hem the short ends. Fold in half lengthwise with right sides together and stitch to make a tube.

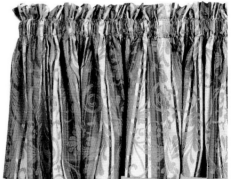

2 Turn right side out and press with the seam to the back of the valance. Measure and mark the casing for the valance track; this should be twice the depth of the track. Make sure the casing does not line up with the seam on the back. Stitch along both marked seams.

3 Insert the track into the casing, pushing the fabric along to evenly distribute the gathers, and mount to the wall. The finished valance is doubled so the right side of the fabric shows on both sides.

GATHERED VARIATIONS

Simple gathered valances on tracks are useful for hiding the mechanism that operates blinds, but they can also make the top edge of a plain curtain more interesting. These valances can be made to any size, and the heading ruffle and skirt can be large or small. A special extra-wide track, onto which a valance with a wide casing can be used, is available, and valances can also be made like curtains using heading tape (see pages 106–9).

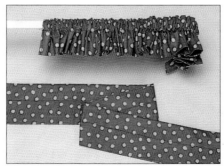

Above: *This valance has been made in the same way as the gathered valances, above, but the casing is measured from the top edge and only one seam has been stitched. There is no ruffle above the track, only a skirt below it.*

Above: *The technique used to make this valance is also the same as the gathered valance, but the casing is centered in the middle of the doubled fabric strip. The heading ruffle and the skirt are the same depth.*

Swags and Tie-backs

SWAGS ARE HEMMED LENGTHS of fabric that drape around a window to give the effect of a curtain. They are often used to soften the look of a window covered by a blind or shutters, and usually hang from poles or wall-mounted hooks. Hang the fabric first before cutting to estimate length and width. Tie-backs, designed to hold a curtain back when open, can be made in any shape or style.

Simple hooks for swags

Coil swag hook

Hardware
Although there are hooks designed specifically to hold swags, many other types can be used.

Curtain hook

Simple Swag

1 *Measure and cut a length of fabric for the swag. Level the fabric and trim selvedges (see Useful Tip, right). Turn under and hem all four edges, backstitching over the corners.*

2 *This swag is made from a lightweight printed cotton fabric that drapes beautifully. It has been hung from wall-mounted swag brackets, available from specialist curtain departments.*

USEFUL TIP

To level the cut edge on printed fabric, lay the fabric flat. Fold it lengthwise to align and match the pattern. Mark a straight line across the width. Pin the layers together and trim along the marked line.

Reversible Swag

1 *Measure and cut two pieces of fabric to the same size. Level and trim selvedges (see Useful Tip). With right sides together, pin and stitch the pieces together, leaving a 6-in (15-cm) gap.*

2 *Finish raw edges, clip corners and turn the swag right sides out. Push the corners out carefully and press. Slipstitch the gap closed.*

3 *This reversible swag has been wrapped around a wooden pole and hangs from each end so one pattern of fabric is seen along the top and the other forms the drape.*

Basic Tie-back

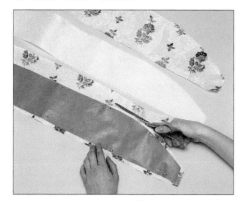

1 *Assess the length of the tie-back by measuring around the curtain to the wall-mounted hook. Make a paper pattern to the desired shape and size. For each tie-back, cut one iron-on interfacing piece to the size of the pattern and two fabric pieces to the pattern plus seams.*

2 *Iron the interfacing onto the wrong side of one fabric piece. With right sides together, stitch the fabric pieces together around all edges, using the interfacing as a stitching guide. Leave a gap for turning, then clip corners.*

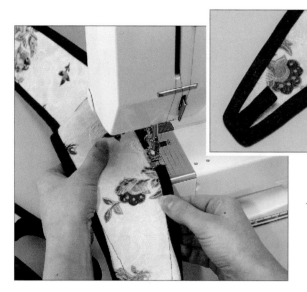

3 *Turn right side out and press. Slipstitch the gap closed. Stitch bias binding around all edges on the back of the tie-back, then fold it to the front (see page 45). Topstitch the binding in place on the front. Inset: At each end of the tie-back, stitch in a fabric loop on the right side .*

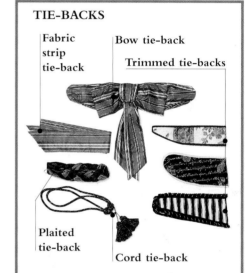

TIE-BACKS

Fabric strip tie-back

Bow tie-back

Trimmed tie-backs

Plaited tie-back

Cord tie-back

Decorative lace, fringe or other trims can be added to simple tie-backs, but tie-backs can also be made from other materials, such as a cord with tassels or a large stiffened bow. A plain hemmed fabric strip, or three strips plaited together, can be tied around a curtain.

Twisted Cord Tie-back

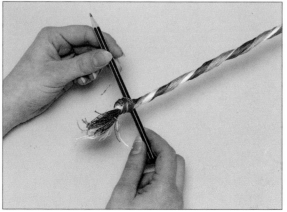

1 *Cut embroidery thread or yarn to three times the desired length of the cord. Tie the ends together at each end.*

2 *Insert a pencil beside the knot at one end and attach the other end to a doorknob or ask someone else to hold it in another pencil. Twist the lengths in one direction until the cord begins to kink.*

3 *Release one end and let the cord wrap around itself from the middle of its length. Join the two loose ends and use as a simple tie-back.*

Blinds

AMONG THE SIMPLEST of window coverings
are blinds, sometimes called window shades.
Roller blinds are easy to make using a kit,
and kits are available in a variety of sizes
from curtain outlets and department stores.
Roman blinds are pleated when open, but
lie flat when closed. Austrian or balloon
blinds are lightweight and frilly, perfect for a
bedroom or room in a period style.
Information about measuring a window for
curtains on page 102 also applies to blinds.

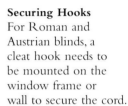

Pull Cords
Decorative finials
for pull cords on
roller blinds can
be purchased, but
you may prefer to
make your own, such as the
tassel shown on page 117.

Securing Hooks
For Roman and
Austrian blinds, a
cleat hook needs to
be mounted on the
window frame or
wall to secure the cord.

Roller Blind

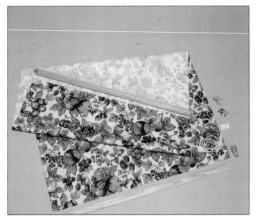

1 Measure, mark and cut a length of fabric
according to the kit guidelines and the
measurement of the window. Check the kit to
make sure it contains a spring roller, a bottom
slat, cord and small pieces of hardware.

2 Turn under, pin and machine-stitch a
narrow hem on both sides of the length
of fabric. Zigzag-stitch a single hem at the top
raw edge.

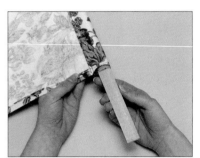

3 Turn up, pin and stitch the
bottom edge to make a casing
wide enough to enclose the wooden
slat. Insert the slat and slipstitch
the ends of the casing.

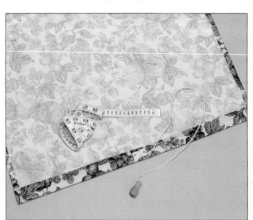

4 Attach the pull cord hardware in the
center of the back of the slat, following
the kit instructions. Thread a finial on the
cord and knot the end. If desired, apply a
coat of protective spray-on fabric stiffener.

5 Attach the top edge of the fabric to the
spring roller carefully. This roller has a
self-adhesive strip onto which the fabric is
pressed. Secure the fabric with staples or small
nails if desired.

6 Mount the brackets on the
window frame or wall. Roll up
the blind and insert the prongs
into the brackets. Pull the blind to
set the mechanism.

Decorative Finishes

Plain roller blinds can be finished with imagination and style. All the ideas shown here can be executed easily, or used to spark off your own ideas. Tassels, as shown below, can be used as finials on pull cords or sewn onto the edge of a blind.

TECHNIQUES

	page
Bindings and Borders	44
Curtains	102
Hems	64
Mitering	41
Pleats	43
Stitches	32

Simple Edges

The top blind has a simple edging of wide cotton lace, which was applied after the bottom casing was sewn. The sides of the bottom blind are bound in dark blue piping, and a perky bow was sewn in the center of the slat.

Scalloped Edge
A scalloped edge was made into the faced fabric, then topstitched (see page 105). The casing is made from a separate strip of fabric sewn on the back of the blind.

Pointed Edge
This border makes effective use of the fabric pattern. The edges can be cut wide enough for hemming, or a facing can be applied, as left. A separate casing is sewn on the back.

Pleated Edge
A doubled strip of fabric has been box-pleated (see pages 43 and 113) and then applied to the bottom of the casing to make a stylish tailored edge.

Tasselled Edge
A length of tasselled fringe, available from upholstery and furnishing departments, has been applied to the bottom edge of the blind after the casing was made.

Making a Tassel

1 Cut a piece of cardboard to twice the desired length of the tassel. Fold it in half and wrap embroidery thread or yarn around until the tassel is the desired thickness.

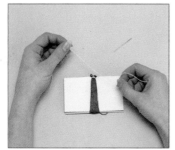

2 Using a blunt needle, pull another thread under the wrapped threads at the folded end. Wrap around several times, pulling tightly, and knot to secure the thread.

3 Slide a pair of scissors carefully into the open edge of the cardboard and cut through the wrapped threads. Do not cut through the top of the tassel.

4 Wrap a new thread around the top of the tassel to make a 'neck'. Tie off tightly and thread the ends up through the top of the tassel to make a cord. Trim the bottom edge.

Roman Blind

A Roman blind, or shade, looks very similar to a roller blind when closed. However, it is finished at the back with three or more strips of special looped fabric tape, which makes the fabric fall into neat pleats when the blind is pulled up. The pull cords are tied together at one side and can be wound around a cleat hook when the blind is up. The blind fabric should measure the length and width of the window, plus the depth of the bottom casing, hems and any seam allowances.

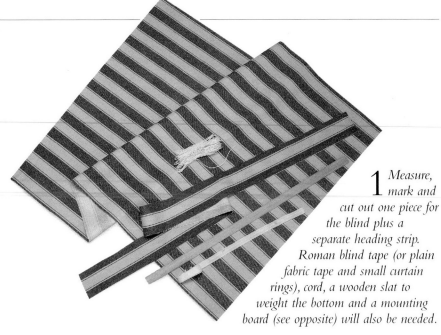

1 *Measure, mark and cut out one piece for the blind plus a separate heading strip. Roman blind tape (or plain fabric tape and small curtain rings), cord, a wooden slat to weight the bottom and a mounting board (see opposite) will also be needed.*

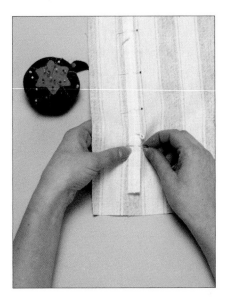

2 *Mark guidelines for the vertical tapes in at least three places – each side and center – depending on the width of the window. Pin the tape in place covering the marked lines, then stitch each tape along both long edges. Avoid catching the loops in the stitching.*

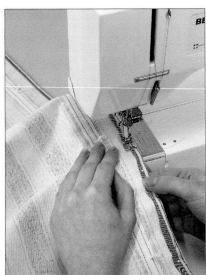

3 *Turn under, pin and stitch a narrow double hem along each side edge of the length of fabric.*

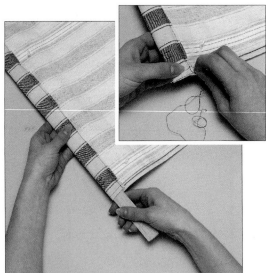

4 *Turn up the bottom edge and stitch a casing to hold the wooden slat, as for step 3 of the roller blind on page 116. Slide the slat inside the casing. Inset: Slipstitch the ends of the casting closed to secure the slat.*

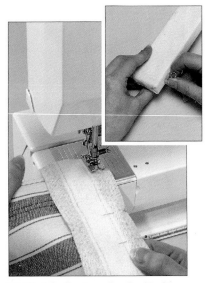

5 *Finish the top edge by binding it with the heading strip (see page 45). Inset: On one narrow edge of the mounting board, screw in an eye to align with each vertical length of tape.*

6 *Using a staple gun or nails, secure the top bound edge of the blind to the side of the mounting board that will rest against the wall. Wrap the blind over to hang down the front of the board.*

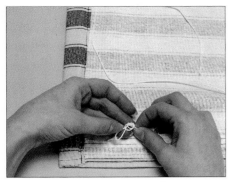

7 Slip the end of a length of cord into the bottom loop or ring on one of the side lengths of vertical tape and knot it securely to attach.

8 Thread the cord up through each loop in the tape. At the top, leave enough extra cord to stretch across the width of the blind. Repeat for each vertical tape, working from one side to the other.

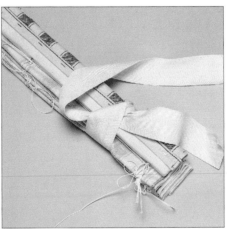

9 Thread the top of each length of cord through the screw eyes in the edge of the mounting board in one direction. Bring all the cords through the eyes from one side to the other, knotting them together at the edge. Trim, then attach a separate length of cord securely to the knotted ends to make a pull cord.

10 Fold the tape into accordian (concertina) pleats, aligning the tape loops, and tie with cotton tape at each end. Leave wrapped to set the folds.

11 To mount the finished blind, screw through the mounting board directly into the window frame or wall; alternatively, mount the board on brackets. Mount a cleat hook on the pull-cord side. The matching valance shown here covers the top of the window and reduces light and draughts.

Making a Mounting Board

A plain piece of wood can be used to mount a blind, but covering it in fabric makes the top of the blind look neater and protects the blind from wear along the folds where it wraps around the board.

To make the board, cut a piece of 2- x 1-in (5- x 2.5-cm) wood to the desired length. Measure all around the width of the board, including all sides. Cut a piece of lining fabric to that width plus seam allowances; the length of the fabric should measure the length of the board plus 2 in (5 cm) at each end (see right, top).

Fold the fabric in half lengthwise and sew the long edges. Turn right side out. Slide the board inside the fabric tube and turn the ends inside neatly. Miter the corners and slipstitch to secure the ends (see right, bottom).

Austrian Blind

Also known as a balloon shade, this ruched blind combines characteristics of both curtains and Roman blinds. An ordinary curtain heading is usually found across the top. The back of the blind is stitched with rows of tape similar to that used on Roman blinds but without the loops.

The width of the fabric for the blind should measure the width of the window, multiplied by 2 to 2½, plus side seams and seam allowances for joining sections if necessary. The length of the fabric should measure the length of the window, multiplied by 2 to 2½, plus hems. Allow more if using lightweight fabric than for heavier weights.

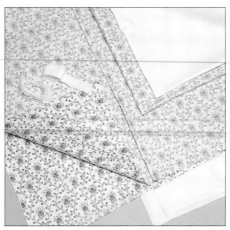
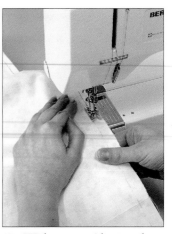

1 *Measure, mark and cut the front piece, joining sections to make up the width. Cut out a lining piece to the same measurement, less 2 in (5 cm) on the width. Austrian blind shirring tape, curtain rings, heading tape and cord are also needed.*

2 *With wrong sides together, pin and stitch the front and lining pieces together along the two side edges.*

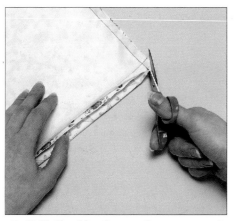

3 *Fold the side edges so they are turned back evenly. Press the seam allowance toward the outside edge. Pin and stitch the front to the lining along the bottom edge, then clip the corners.*

4 *Turn the blind right side out through the top. Press the blind carefully, making sure that the turned-back edges are equal on both sides.*

5 *Turn up a single hem along the bottom edge, mitering the corners (see page 41), and pin in place. Slipstitch the hem to secure.*

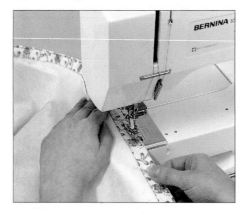

6 *To create a neat and attractive finished edge to the blind, topstitch along the two side edges and the bottom hemmed edge.*

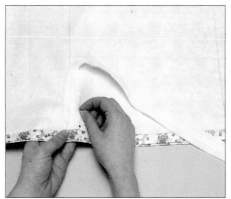

7 *Mark vertical guidelines for the shirring tape on the lining at regular intervals. Pin lengths of tape in place over the marked lines, turning both ends of each length of tape under as shown.*

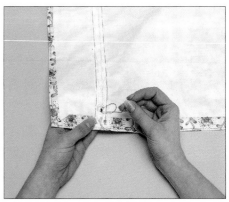

8 *Stitch each length of tape in place along both long edges. Sew a series of curtain rings at regular intervals along each tape, lining up the rings evenly across the width of the blind.*

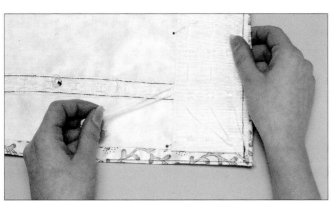

9 *Finish the top edge of the blind by turning under ¹/₂ in (1.5 cm) and pinning, then stitching the top edge of the heading tape to cover the raw edges (see page 106). Pull the ends of the cords in the shirring tape clear of the heading tape.*

10 *Pin and stitch the lower edge of the heading tape in place. Inset: Take care to avoid catching the ends of the shirring tape cord in the seam.*

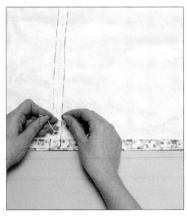

11 *Cut a piece of cord measuring the length plus the width of the finished blind, plus an extra 6 in (15 cm). Tie the cord to the bottom ring on one strip of shirring tape. Repeat to tie cord on each tape.*

12 *Pull up the gathering cords on each length of shirring tape until the desired finished length is reached. Thread each cord attached in step 11 through each ring along its tape, knotting securely. Thread the cords through the top rings in one direction, knot them all together on one side and attach a pull cord, as for steps 8 and 9 of the Roman Blind (see page 119).*

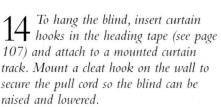

13 *Pull up the heading tape to the desired width of the blind and tie the ends of the cords securely (see page 107). Even up the vertical ruching and the heading gathers.*

14 *To hang the blind, insert curtain hooks in the heading tape (see page 107) and attach to a mounted curtain track. Mount a cleat hook on the wall to secure the pull cord so the blind can be raised and lowered.*

Tablecloths

TABLE LINEN CAN BE EXPENSIVE to buy and difficult to find in the size, shape and color you need. To make tablecloths, all you need is a few hours of time and a working area large enough to lay out the fabric.

Making square or rectangular tablecloths can be a simple matter of measuring, cutting and hemming a length of fabric. Accurate measuring is crucial. First measure the length and width of the tabletop, then add the length of the drop, or overhang, and hems; remember that the overhang and hems must be doubled on both the length and width.

For a circular tablecloth, use the measurement of the desired diameter of the circle, including drops and hems. For oval tablecloths, measure as for a rectangular tablecloth, but fold the rectangle into quarters and round off the corner to the desired curve, as described for the circular tablecloth below.

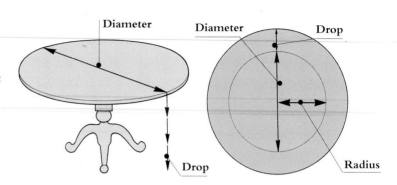

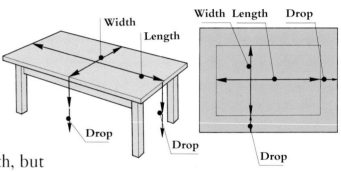

Circular Tablecloth

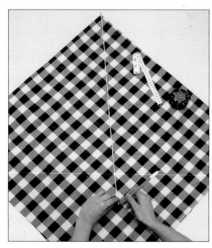

1 *Measure and cut a square of fabric to the desired diameter of the circle, including hems. Fold in quarters and pin the edges. Cut a length of string measuring the radius of the desired circle plus hems and pin it in the folded corner. Mark a quarter-circle using the string as a guide.*

2 *Carefully cut along the marked line through all four layers of fabric. Unpin and open out the circular tablecloth.*

3 *Pin a double hem all around, close to the edge, and stitch it in place (see page 64).*

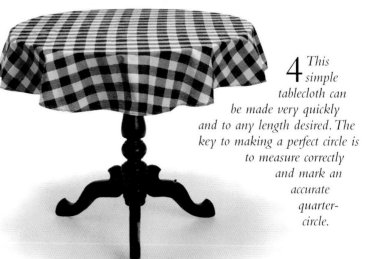

4 *This simple tablecloth can be made very quickly and to any length desired. The key to making a perfect circle is to measure correctly and mark an accurate quarter-circle.*

Wide Circular Tablecloth

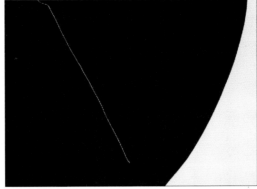

1 *Cut two pieces of fabric to the desired length of the tablecloth, including drops and hems. Fold one piece in half lengthwise, matching selvedges. Pin, then cut along the fold to make two pieces the same length as the main fabric, but only half as wide.*

2 *Stitch each narrower piece of fabric to an outside edge of the main piece. Make sure the width measurement is correct, trimming both sides if necessary. Fold, mark and cut the fabric to make a circle as described in steps 1 and 2 of the Circular Tablecloth.*

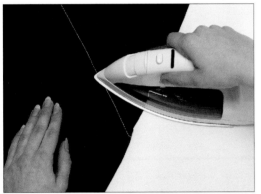

4 *With this method of joining fabric sections, unsightly seams down the middle of the tablecloth are avoided. This technique can also be used for making large oval or rectangular tablecloths that cannot be cut from one piece of fabric.*

3 *Press the seams to the outside edges of the tablecloth. Turn up and pin a double hem and stitch it in place to finish the tablecloth, as in step 3 of the Circular Tablecloth, opposite.*

USEFUL TIP

When joining lengths of printed fabric for tablecloths, you may want to match the pattern exactly to make the seam less visible. This technique of matching patterns can also be used for other sewing projects, such as making curtains, cushions or garments.

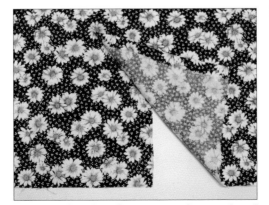

1 *Trim the edge of one piece to be joined and press ¹/2 in (1.25 cm) to the wrong side. Lay the second piece flat and match the folded edge of the first piece to the pattern on the second piece. Pin in place along the matching point on the right side.*

2 *Working on the wrong side and moving the pins carefully as you work, fold the fabric back and stitch the seam. Use the folded edge as a stitching guide. The seam is now virtually invisible.*

TABLECLOTH EDGES *Lace Insert Border*

While plain hemmed tablecloths are neat and elegant, adding decorative trimmings and edgings can turn an ordinary piece into an item suitable for special celebrations or nice enough to give as a gift. Tablecloths can be fringed or decorated with braid. They can be embellished with embroidery all around the edges and in the center, or stitched only in the corners. Use your imagination to create your own individual designs.

1 *Measure and cut the main fabric piece to the desired square (see page 122). Cut four wide border strips, joining lengths if necessary, and four lengths of lace.*

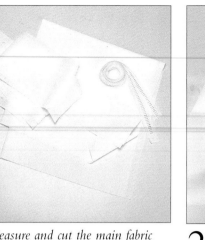

2 *With right sides together, pin and stitch a length of lace to the raw edge of the main fabric. Work around the cloth one side at a time, leaving an end of unstitched surplus lace at each corner.*

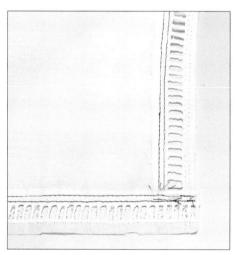

3 *Turn the lace out, press it flat and topstitch the seam to finish and secure it. As you topstitch, join the overlapping end of the lace to the end of the adjoining strip, here shown from the wrong side.*

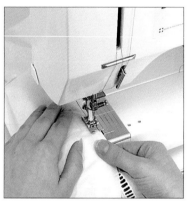

4 *With right sides together, pin and stitch the border pieces to the raw edge of lace all around. Leave overlaps at each corner to correspond with the corners of the lace.*

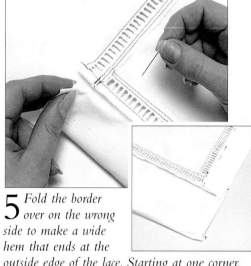

5 *Fold the border over on the wrong side to make a wide hem that ends at the outside edge of the lace. Starting at one corner, pin the edge. Inset: At the next corner, fold a narrow hem inside the end of the second border strip and pin it in place.*

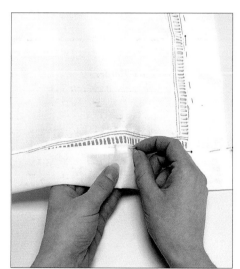

6 *Continue pinning along the second side, folding up a deep double hem as before. Repeat steps 5 and 6 for all the corners.*

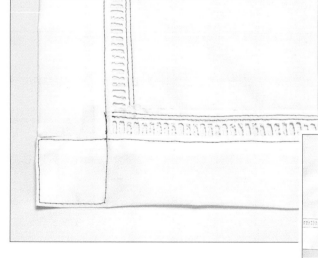

7 *Topstitch all sides of the tablecloth to finish the border hem, stitching a square around each corner as shown. Inset: The wrong side is almost as neat as the right side.*

Satin-stitched Scalloped Edge

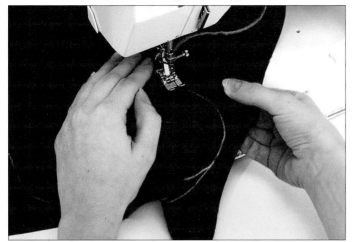

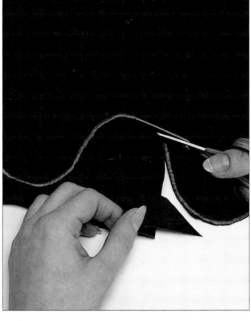

1 Cut the fabric to the desired size and level the edges. Make a template of the scallops from cardboard (see page 105) and mark around the template onto the edge of the fabric; alternatively, draw a freehand decorative edge. Satin-stitch through one layer of fabric, following the marked line all around.

2 Trim carefully along the outside edge of the stitched line. Cut as closely as possible but take care not to cut into the stitches themselves.

3 Scalloped edges are decorative and give a lift to a simple cloth underneath. Simple cardboard templates can be made in any shape, from deep curves like these to pointed triangles. Paper patterns of decorative borders can also be purchased.

OTHER DECORATIVE EDGES

Bound Edge
Any tablecloth can be edged with bias binding, either matching as shown here or contrasting. Cut the fabric edges to the size and shape of the finished tablecloth and apply the binding (see page 45).

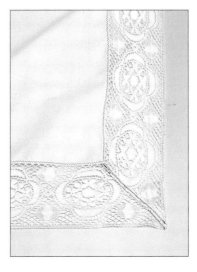

Lace Border
To make a delicate lace border, trim the fabric to size and turn under a single hem along all edges. Pin the lace to the fabric and apply it using a zigzag stitch that also finishes the seam. Here a flat fell seam (see page 37) has been used in the corner miters (see page 41).

Napkins and Runners

SMALL PIECES OF TABLE LINEN are easier to make than tablecloths and can be embellished with attractive trims and borders. Extra napkins are always useful and can be matched to other linen. The hem-stitched napkin below is worked on fine evenweave linen, while the plain version is made from inexpensive sheeting, though you may like to use a fine-quality linen.

Runners can vary in size from small traycloths to narrow sweeps of fabric that cover the middle of a long table. Small padded pieces that protect bare wooden tabletops can also be made.

Plain Napkin

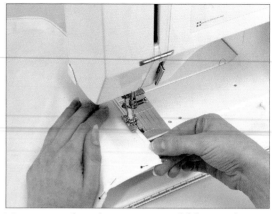

Measure, mark and cut a square of fabric to the desired size, plus hems. Turn under, pin and stitch a narrow double hem. At the corners, stop with the needle in the fabric, lift the presser foot and turn the fabric (see page 36).

Napkin with Mitered Corners

1 *Measure, mark and cut fabric as for the plain napkin, but allowing for a deep double hem. Fold the corner with wrong sides together and stitch a miter (see page 41). Clip the corner. Repeat for all corners.*

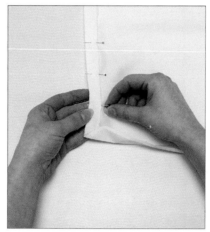

2 *Turn the miters right side out and press the edges. Turn under and pin a narrow hem along the raw edge. Stitch in place from the right side.*

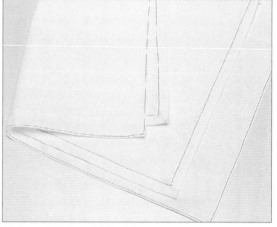

Plain and Mitered Napkins
Both plain and mitered edges make a neat finish for napkins, as shown here. The wrong side of the mitered napkin is shown in the center.

Hem-stitched Napkin

1 *Measure, mark and cut the fabric. Hem and miter the corners (see page 41). Mark and baste all the rows of hemstitching, as shown. You may need to count threads to make sure the rows are even.*

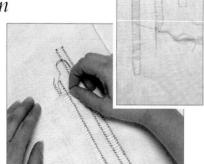

2 *Cut lengthwise threads in the center of one row. Use a blunt needle to tease the threads out, withdrawing them to the marked edge. Inset: Trim and weave them back in as shown, repeating for each row.*

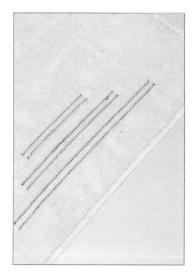

3 *Fasten the stitching thread at the left-hand end of a row and weave under four threads from right to left. Loop the thread around and take the needle, from back to front, two threads below the bottom of the row of withdrawn threads on the right of the loop. Continue, working along the top and bottom of each row.*

Plain Runner

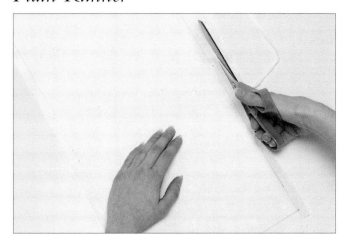

1 Measure and mark the hem foldline on the fabric. Trim the edges of the fabric evenly 3/4 in (15 mm) from the marked line.

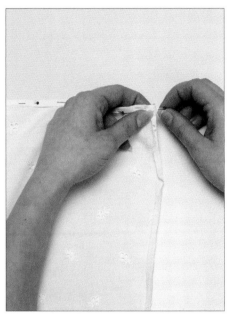

2 Turn under and pin a narrow double hem along the foldline. Stitch in place.

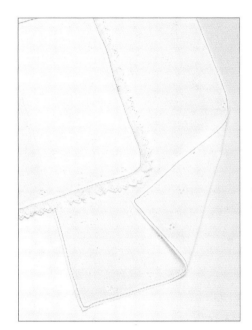

3 The finished runner has been stitched in a contrasting color for clarity. A decorative edging can be added to the hemmed runner, as shown here on a traycloth made from the same fabric as the runner.

Padded Reversible Runner

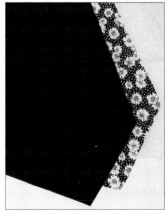

1 Measure, mark and cut two pieces of fabric, one plain and one patterned, and one piece of batting (wadding), all the same size. The pieces should measure the desired size of the runner, plus seam allowances all around.

2 With right sides of the fabric together and the batting on the bottom, pin all three layers. Stitch around the edges, leaving a 4-in (10-cm) gap for turning.

3 Clip all corners, or curves, and turn the runner right side out through the gap. Press to align all edges, then slipstitch the gap closed.

4 Further decoration can be added to the edge. Simple topstitching, (top) or a braid trim, (bottom) are just two ideas.

Placemats

PLACEMATS CAN BE AS SIMPLE as two pieces of fabric stitched together with a layer of batting (wadding) in between, or as ornate and elegant as you desire. Made in sets with matching napkins, they are ideal personalized presents for a bride or someone moving into a new home.

Reversible Placemat

1 Pin two pieces of fabric with right sides together. On the top piece, mark the shape and size of the finished placemat. Trim 3/4 in (15 mm) from the marked line all around for the seam allowance.

2 Stitch along the marked line, leaving a 4-in (10-cm) gap for turning the placemat right side out. Clip the corners and any curves.

3 Turn the placemat right side out through the gap and press carefully to straighten the edges. Neatly slipstitch the gap closed.

4 Repeat steps 1 to 3 to make as many placemats as required. The finished mats can be used on either side, or try alternating them around a table setting.

Quilted Placemat

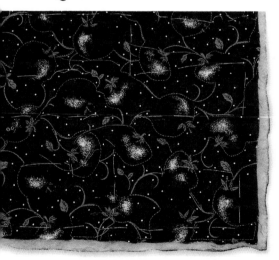

1 Cut out two pieces of fabric and one of batting (wadding) to the desired size plus seam allowances. With wrong sides of the fabric together and batting in the middle, baste all layers before quilting (see page 100). Alternatively, use ready-quilted fabric cut to size.

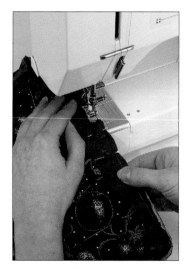

2 Apply bias binding all around the edge (see page 45), taking care to stitch through all layers and finish the stitching neatly on the right side.

3 The finished placemats are lightly padded and neatly bound. This method can be used to make decorative pot holders with multiple layers of batting (wadding).

Appliqué Placemat

1 Measure and cut two pieces of fabric and one of batting (wadding) to the desired size of the placemat, allowing 3/4 in (15 mm) extra all around for a seam allowance.

2 Make appliqué templates from cardboard. Iron the glue side of fusible webbing to the wrong side of the fabric pieces to be used for the appliqué. Draw around the templates onto the webbing backing papers and cut out the shapes.

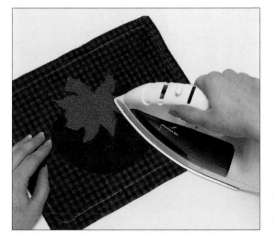

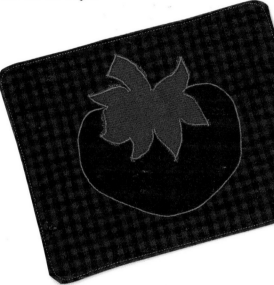

3 Position the paper-backed appliqué pieces on the right side of the top fabric. When the design is arranged, remove the backing paper on each piece, one by one, and press in place following the manufacturer's instructions.

4 When all the appliqué pieces are fused in place, satin-stitch all around each piece to finish the edges. Make sure that all raw edges are stitched down.

5 To finish each placemat, follow steps 2 and 3 for the Reversible Placemat, placing the fabric pieces with right sides together and the batting piece on top. Topstitch around all sides if desired.

Self-bound Placemat

1 Measure and cut one piece of fabric for the top and one of batting (wadding) to the finished size of the placemat. Cut the backing fabric 1–2 in (2.5–5 cm) larger all around. Pin and baste the top and batting together and quilt as desired (see page 100). Pin the quilted top to the wrong side of the backing fabric, centered. Turn under and pin a hem along the raw edge, mitering the corners.

2 Topstitch along all four turned-under edges, removing pins as you work. The turned-up edge of the backing fabric becomes the binding on the finished placemat.

Cushions

Circular Cushion with Overlap Closure

CUSHIONS, OR THROW pillows, and circular bolsters are among the easiest of home furnishings to sew, and can make a decorative statement in the home. Pads, or forms, to fill cushion covers can be purchased for reasonable prices, but are also simple to make in almost any shape (see page 132). Techniques for making covers for seating, such as box cushions, are also included in this section.

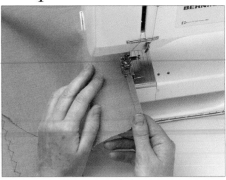

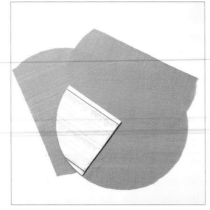

1 *Make a paper pattern to the desired size plus seam allowances and use it to cut three circles from the fabric. Trim away approximately one-third of two of the fabric circles, as shown; these will make up the overlapping back piece.*

2 *Fold back, press and herringbone-stitch a deep single hem on the raw straight edges of one backing piece. Turn under and machine-stitch a double hem on the straight edge of the second backing piece.*

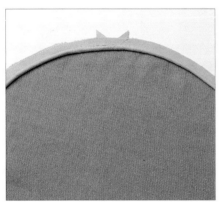

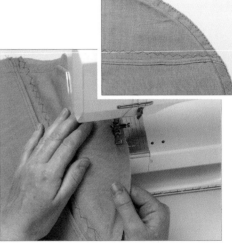

3 *Apply piping (see page 46) to the edge of the front circular piece with raw edges aligned all around. Make sure the cord lies just outside the seam allowance. Join the ends of the piping (see Useful Tip, below).*

4 *Pin and baste all three pieces with right sides together. Layer the pieces as shown, with the front piece on the bottom, then the herringboned piece and finally the machine-hemmed piece.*

5 *Stitch all around the circular cushion. Work as close to the corded piping as possible, but do not stitch over the cord. Inset: Zigzag to finish the seam and trim the raw edge.*

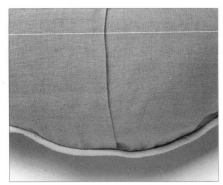

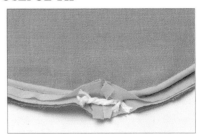

6 *Turn the cushion cover right sides out through the overlapped back and insert a cushion pad. The piping finishes the edge neatly and the overlap makes removing the cover easy.*

Fillers
The most popular fillings for cushions are (clockwise): feathers, usually duck or goose; kapok, a soft vegetable fiber; synthetic fiberfill stuffing; and styrofoam balls or pellets, used in beanbags.

USEFUL TIP

To join the ends of a length of piping, allow about 1 in (2.5 cm) of overlap. Turn back the fabric about 1 in (2.5 cm) at each end. Twist the cord ends together and fold back one fabric end. Turn under a small hem on the other end and slipstitch to the piping.

Zipped Square Cushion

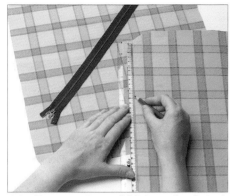

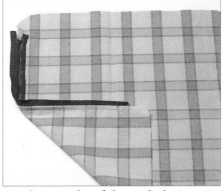

1 *Cut two pieces of fabric to the desired size plus seam allowances. Mark a seamline on the wrong side of one piece 1/2 in (1.25 cm) from the edge. You will need a zipper 2 in (5 cm) shorter than one side of the finished cushion.*

2 *On one edge of the marked piece, pin, baste and stitch the zipper in place, centered on the seam as shown, backstitching at both short ends to secure (see page 76).*

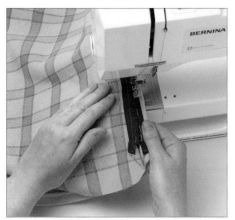

3 *If desired, apply piping or another trim to the second, unmarked piece (see page 46). Baste and stitch the other side of the zipper to one edge of the piped piece with the piping cord resting against the teeth, as shown.*

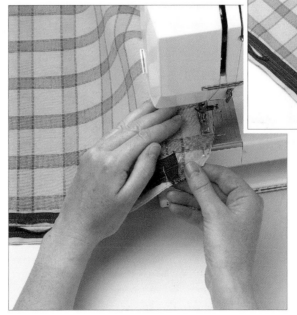

4 *With the zipper open and right sides facing, pin and stitch the two pieces together, stopping just before the zipper is reached. Finish the seam with zigzag stitching. Inset: Fold back the seam allowance at each end of the zipper and stitch to secure, backstitching the ends to reinforce.*

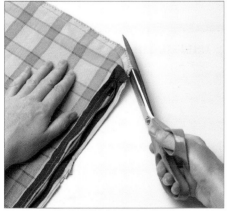

5 *Trim the seam allowance, taking care not to cut through the zigzag stitches. Turn the cushion cover right sides out through the zipper and insert a pad.*

Square and Circular Cushions
The finished covers show two different methods for openings. The zipper and overlap techniques are interchangeable and work for most cushion shapes.

USEFUL TIP

Gently round off the corners on a square cushion when cutting out the fabric pieces. This will help achieve a more attractive finish, particularly with those cushions that have a decorative edge, such as piping or a ruffle.

SHAPED CUSHIONS

Making cushions in geometric shapes, such as circles, squares, diamonds and triangles, is straightforward, but for more complicated shapes you will need to make a pattern for both the pad and the cover from either brown paper or newspaper. The pattern for the cover will need to be slightly larger than the pattern for the pad. Allow ¼ in (6mm) all around for the cover.

Paper Patterns
Draw and cut to size a pattern of the shape you want, including seam allowances all around. If the shape is symmetrical, fold pattern in half to ensure measurements are correct.

Heart-shaped Cushion Pad

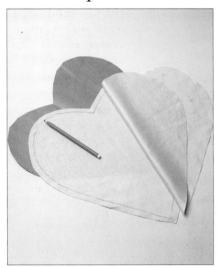

1 *Make a paper pattern for the heart shape. (It should measure the desired size of the cushion cover plus the seam allowances all around.) Use the pattern to cut out two pieces of heavy lining fabric. Mark the seamline on one piece.*

2 *With right sides facing, pin and stitch the two pieces together, leaving a 4-in (10-cm) gap for turning and stuffing. Clip corners and curves as necessary.*

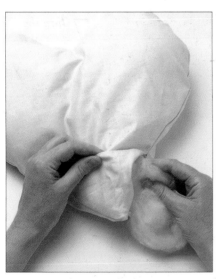

3 *Turn right side out and press. Stuff the pad to the desired fullness using a filler (see page 130). If you are using feathers, make sure the fabric is featherproof; alternatively you can use two layers of fabric for the pad so that the feathers do not slip through. Slipstitch the gap closed.*

4 *The finished pad is ready to be inserted into a heart-shaped cushion cover. This technique can be used to make any shape of cushion pad.*

Heart-shaped Cover with Ties

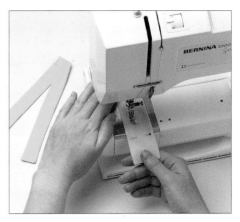

1 Cut a paper pattern to the desired shape plus seams. Fold in half, then fold a generous overlap. Cut one piece for the front using the full pattern. Fold the pattern to the overlap and use to cut two back pieces. Mark the seamline on the front piece. Mark the center foldline on the back pieces.

2 Measure two long strips for the ties to the desired length and width. The ties shown here measure $2^{1}/_{2}$ x 14 in (6 x 35 cm). Mark seamlines, then cut out the ties, allowing for seams.

3 Fold a tie in half lengthwise with right sides together and pin. Stitch one short end and the long edge along the marked seamline. Turn right sides out and press. Repeat for the second tie.

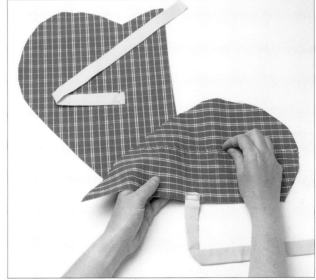

5 Finish the raw straight edges on the back pieces. To do this, fold the overlap piece along the marked center foldline and herringbone-stitch the raw edge in place. Turn under and machine-stitch a narrow double hem on the underlap piece. Pin the ties in place at the basted points, turning raw short ends under, and stitch in place.

4 Mark the position of the ties on the back pieces with basting. The tie on the overlap piece is positioned on the foldline. The tie on the underlap piece is positioned where the two sides meet.

6 Place the back pieces on the front piece with right sides together, aligning the overlap carefully. Pin and stitch around the heart, taking care to avoid stitching over ties.

7 Turn the cushion cover right side out and insert the pad. A tied bow makes a pretty closure.

DECORATIVE TECHNIQUES

Use ingenuity to add interesting decoration to simple shapes of cushions. The techniques shown here for applying various trims, edgings and fancy details will help you with your own ideas.

Cushion with Cord Edge

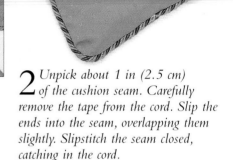

1 To add ready-made cord to a finished cushion cover, first wrap one end of the cord with masking tape. Stitch the cord around the edge, taking a stitch through the cord and another through the fabric. At the join, wrap masking tape around the remaining end, allowing for an overlap. Inset: Cut through the tape.

2 Unpick about 1 in (2.5 cm) of the cushion seam. Carefully remove the tape from the cord. Slip the ends into the seam, overlapping them slightly. Slipstitch the seam closed, catching in the cord.

Fringed Cushion

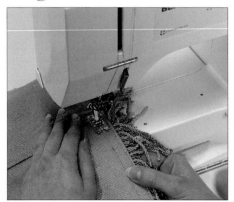

1 Pin the fringe all around the edge of the front of a cushion cover. Baste if necessary, then stitch in place. Because this fringe is fairly heavy and has a wide heading, it was stitched along both the top and the bottom of the heading.

2 The stitching lines are not visible on the right side because the fringe has a heavyweight plaited heading.

3 For a distinctly period feel, knot two or more strands of fringe together, continuing around the edge of the cushion cover. The knots have been finished tightly against the heading.

Buttoned Cushion

1 Make the cushion from two identical fabric pieces in the same way as for a cushion pad, slipstitching the gap closed (see page 132). Do not stuff the cushion too full. Thread an upholstery needle with a long length of doubled thread.

2 Sew a button securely in the middle of one side. Push the needle through to the other side and thread on another button. Pull up tightly to tuft the cushion, then go back through the first button. Repeat several times, then fasten off.

3 The finished cushion has an attractive roundness. The same technique can be used for other shapes of cushion.

Tapestry Insert Cushion

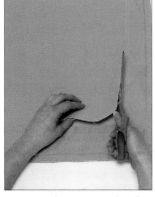

1 *On the wrong side of the front of a finished zipped cover, mark and cut out a window to the size of the tapestry piece, allowing a generous seam allowance all around. Clip as necessary. Open the zipper.*

2 *Press the seam allowance of the window to the wrong side. Press the tapestry canvas and trim any unstitched edges to 1 in (2.5 cm) or less. Pin the canvas to the allowance along all four sides.*

3 *Make sure the edge of the tapestry stitching matches the seamline. Stitch along the seam, carefully backstitching around the corners to reinforce them. Turn right side out through the zipper and insert a pad.*

4 *This technique can be used to display any previously blocked needlework, such as these two companion pieces, to great effect. Panels of needlework – embroidery, patchwork, quilting or appliqué – can also be inserted by hand if you prefer.*

Gingham Cross Stitch Cushion

Cross stitch is a clever way to liven up inexpensive gingham check. Here a green embroidery thread was used in the white squares to make a simple border with corner motifs.

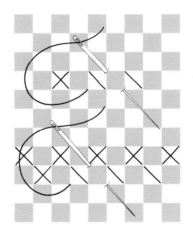

Cross Stitch
Make a row of diagonal stitches from corner to corner in boxes of the same color, then work back along the row in the opposite direction as shown.

Ruffled Cushion

Tie Cushions

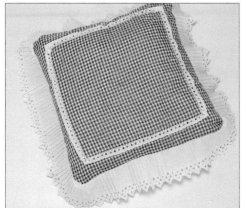

Both these cushions have been made using the overlapped closure (see page 130) and tied with decorative ribbons to keep the opening secured neatly. Ideas for ties are endless, and different colors and patterns can make the ties an eye-catching feature.

The white decoration makes this cushion look crisp and neat. An inner border of lace was sewn on the front piece before the cover was assembled. A ruffle of purchased pleated trim was applied to the edge (see page 47).

Ruffled Tie-on Chair Cushion

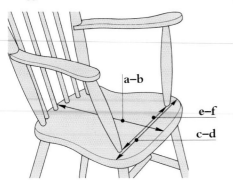

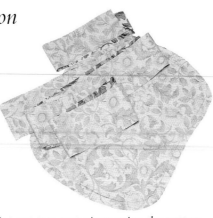

1 *Measure the chair from front to back across the middle (a–b), then across the width at the widest point (c–d) and between the arms (e–f). Make a paper pattern of the seat, adjusting until it is exactly the same size as the chair seat.*

2 *Cut out two seat pieces using the pattern, adding seam allowances. Cut out one ruffle piece; the length measuring 2 to 2½ times the chair sides and front, and the width measuring the desired ruffle depth plus seam allowance and hem. Cut out four ties. Mark seamlines on the wrong side of one seat piece and the ties.*

3 *Make the ties as in steps 2 and 3 of the Heart-Shaped cushion on page 133. Turn right sides out, using a knitting needle if desired. Press the ties.*

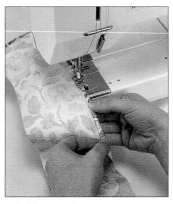

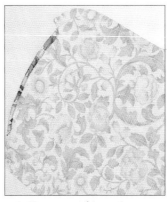

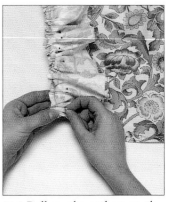

4 *Turn under a narrow double hem on the short ends and one long side of the ruffle piece and stitch. Run a double row of gathering stitches on the remaining long edge (see page 42).*

5 *On the back edge of each cushion piece, turn under and baste a double hem between the points where the ties will be attached. Pin short squares of touch-and-close tape along the hem on each piece, making sure the squares correspond and align.*

6 *On one cushion piece, stitch the touch-and-close pieces in place. Then stitch along the basted hem, securing the turned-under short ends of the hem. Repeat on the second cushion piece.*

7 *Pull up the gathers on the ruffle to the required length. Pin and baste the ruffle along the three raw edges of one cushion piece, with right sides together. Pin and baste two tie pieces, overlapping slightly, at each back corner.*

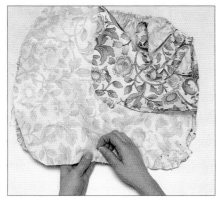

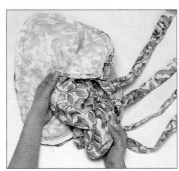

8 *Pin the seat pieces with right sides together. Be sure to keep the ruffle and ties inside of cushion cover, out of the way of the needle.*

9 *Baste and stitch the cushion cover along the sides and front. Turn the cover right side out through the back opening, insert a shaped pad (see page 132) and close the back.*

10 *Tie the cushion around the chair back uprights. The ruffle drapes neatly over the chair seat.*

Bound Tie-on Chair Cushion

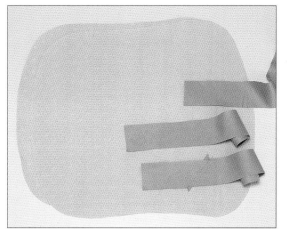

1 Make a pattern for the chair seat as in step 1 for the Ruffled Chair Cushion, opposite. Cut two seat pieces from fabric. From binding, cut two ties, two lengths for the back edges, and one length to go around the whole cover with 24 in (60 cm) over.

2 With right sides together, pin and stitch a binding strip to the raw back edge of a seat piece, between the points where the ties will be joined.

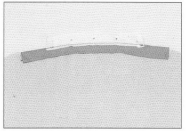

3 Turn the binding to the wrong side, folding under raw edges. Baste in place. Stitch one edge of a length of fastener tape, with the right side facing the wrong side of the cushion, to the folded edge of the binding.

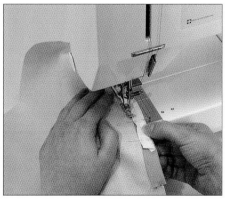

4 Fold back the fastener tape. Pin and stitch along the basted line on the binding. Repeat steps 2, 3 and 4 for the second cushion piece, using the remaining strip of binding for the back section and the corresponding fastener tape.

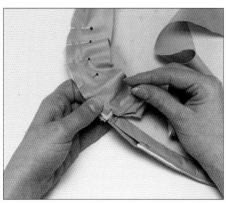

5 Place the cushion pieces with wrong sides together. Pin the long binding strip around the raw edges, leaving 12 in (30 cm) at each end to form ties. Clip into the seam allowance at the back opening. Stitch the binding to the edge.

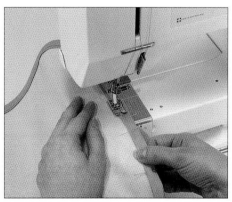

6 Press the binding to the other side. Fold under and pin the raw short ends and along the length, making sure the raw edge is enclosed where the binding meets the cushion. Pin the binding around the seat and stitch from end to end.

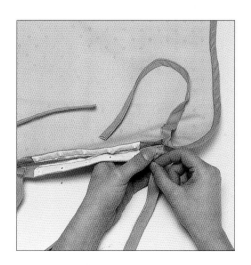

7 Make two separate ties, as in steps 2 and 3 of the Heart-shaped Cushion on page 133. The ties should match the ties sewn into the binding. Pin and stitch the ties to the binding, as shown.

8 Insert the pad, close the back opening and tie the cushion to the chair.

BOX CUSHIONS

Square Zipped Box Cushion

Primarily used as seat cushions, box cushion covers are distinguished from others by a separate strip that makes up the depth of the cushion. Most box cushions use blocks of foam to pad the cushion.

Accurate measuring is important. For square and rectangular cushions, the seat pieces need to be the length and width of the finished cushion plus seam allowances. Three box strips are also needed. One box strip should measure the total of three sides in length and the depth of the cushion pad in width, plus seams on all sides. The remaining two strips, which make up the opening side, should each measure one side of the square or rectangle in length and half the depth of the pad in width, plus seams on all sides.

For circular cushions, the seat pieces need to be the desired diameter of the cushion plus seams. Three box strips are also needed. Two strips should measure half the depth of the pad in width, plus seam allowances, and one strip needs to measure the full depth of the pad in width, plus seams; the strips' length can vary, but must total the circumference of the pad plus any seam allowances.

1 *Cut out two seat pieces, one long box strip and two narrower box strips, following the guidelines on the left. Mark seamlines and corners on the wrong side of all pieces. A zipper that is about 2 in (5 cm) shorter than one side of the cushion is needed.*

2 *With the narrow strips right sides together, stitch each end up to the zipper position. Baste the seam closed. Pin, baste and stitch zipper in the seam on wrong side (see page 76). Remove the basting.*

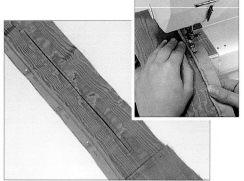

3 *With right sides together, stitch one short end of the long box strip to a short end of the zipper strip. Press the seam open. Inset: Pin the piping on one long edge and stitch in place.*

4 *Repeat to pipe the other edge. Inset: Clip into the seam allowance on both sides of the strip at each marked corner. Stitch the remaining two short ends together. Press seam open and clip the corner.*

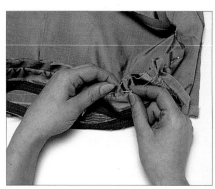

5 *Starting at one corner and with right sides together, pin one seat piece to the piped strip. Pin along the marked seamline, then stitch, turning all corners sharply. Open the zipper. Pin and stitch the second seat piece to the remaining side of the strip.*

6 *Trim the seam allowances and finish with zigzag stitch. Turn the cover right side out through the open zipper and insert the pad.*

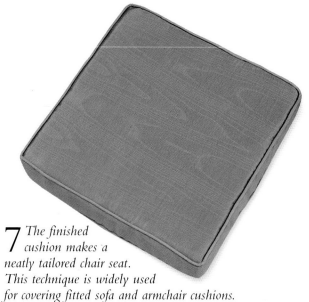

7 *The finished cushion makes a neatly tailored chair seat. This technique is widely used for covering fitted sofa and armchair cushions.*

Bench Cushion

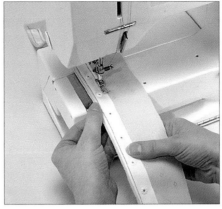

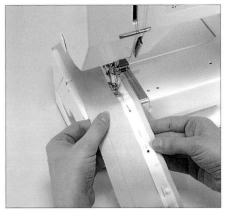

1 Measure, mark and cut two seat pieces, one box strip and two narrow box strips, following the guidelines on page 138. Separate a length of fastener tape and apply to the narrow strips as described in steps 2 and 3, following.

2 Fold a double hem to the right side of one narrow box strip along the length. Pin one half of the fastener tape along the hem, turning under the raw short ends. Stitch along the top and bottom of the hem to secure the tape. The tape appears on the right side.

3 Stitch one long edge of the other half of tape to one long raw edge of the other narrow box strip with right sides together. Fold the tape to the wrong side and pin. Stitch the other tape edge, turning under the short ends. The tape appears on the wrong side.

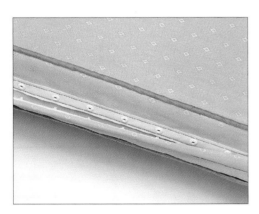

4 Join the fastener tapes and treat strip as one piece. Repeat steps 3 to 6 of the Square Zipped Box Cushion to assemble the cover, making sure the overlapping section of the opening is sewn along the bottom edge of the cushion.

5 The finished cushion makes a bench a more comfortable seating option. Zippers and various fastener tapes can be used interchangeably in boxed cushions.

Easy Square Cushion

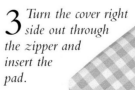

1 Cut two pieces of fabric to the size of the square cushion pad, adding half the depth of the pad and a seam allowance all around. Mark the dimensions of the pad on the wrong side of both pieces. With right sides together, pin and baste one side seam. Insert a zipper in the seam (see page 76).

2 Remove basting and open the zipper. With right sides together, stitch around the remaining three sides. Press the seam open. Stitch across each corner to the depth of the cushion pad, with the seamline centered on each corner seam. Trim the corner seams, as shown.

3 Turn the cover right side out through the zipper and insert the pad.

Piped Circular Box Cushion

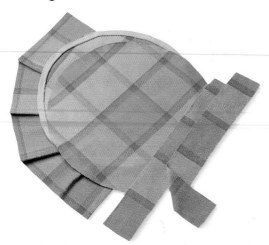

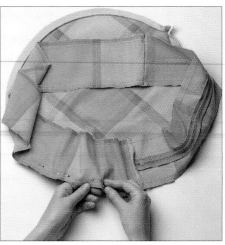

1 Cut two seat pieces, one box strip and two narrow box strips, following the guidelines on page 138. Mark seamlines on the wrong side of all pieces. Pin and stitch a length of piping around the edge of each seat piece (see page 46).

2 Insert a zipper and make the box strip as in steps 4 and 5 of the Square Zipped Box Cushion on page 138. Staystitch 1/2 in (1.25 cm) from each long raw edge, then clip into the seam allowance at 1-in (2.5-cm) intervals.

3 With right sides together, pin the box strip to the raw piped edge of one seat piece, keeping the piping just outside of the seam. Stitch in place.

4 Open the zipper and repeat step 3 to join the second seat piece to the box strip. Trim the seams neatly. Turn the cushion cover right sides out through the zipper and insert the cushion pad.

5 This cushion is perfect for any round-seated chair and would suit kitchen and dining-room chairs, as well as stools.

Simple Circular Box Cushion

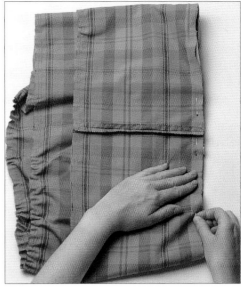

1 Measure the cushion pad. Cut three strips of fabric as long as the circumference of the pad plus seam allowances. The width of one strip should measure the side depth of the cushion pad plus seam allowances. The width of the remaining two strips should measure the radius of the pad plus seam allowances. You also need two buttons or tassels.

2 Fold one of the wide strips in half with right sides facing and stitch across the short ends to make a tube. Repeat for the other wide strip. Press the seams open. Run a double row of gathering stitches along one long raw edge on each strip (see page 42).

3 Apply piping or other decoration to the narrow strip (see page 46), if desired. With right sides together, pin and stitch the ungathered edge of one wide strip to one side of the narrow strip, aligning the seams. Repeat to attach the remaining wide strip.

4 Trim seam allowances and finish the edges with zigzagging. Press the seams toward the outside gathered edges.

5 Pull up the gathers on one side and knot the thread firmly to secure the gathering.

6 Insert the cushion pad carefully and align the edges of the pad with the edges of the center strip. Pull up the gathers on the second side and knot them securely. If necessary, stitch to close the gaps. Sew a button on each side to conceal the gathered edges, or use another form of decoration such as a tassel.

7 The finished cushion cover will give a period feel to a room. To remove the cover for cleaning, snip off the button on one side and loosen the gathers.

BOLSTERS

Bolsters are generally round cylindrical cushions, but they can be long narrow rectangles used, for example, to transform a studio bed or divan into a sofa by day. You can make bolster pads (see page 132) or purchase them. Bolster covers can be elegant or fun, and can be trimmed with piping, cording or fringe in the same way as box cushions. Tassels or buttons can add interest to the center of the flat bolster end.

Gathered Bolster

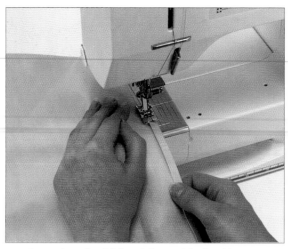

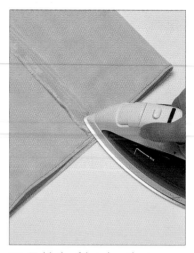

1 *Cut a length of fabric. The width should measure the circumference of the pad plus seams. The length should measure the length of the pad, plus extra for the ruffle, facing and casing at each end. Stitch a narrow double hem on both short ends.*

2 *Fold the fabric lengthwise with right sides together. Pin and stitch the long edge to make a tube. Press the seam open.*

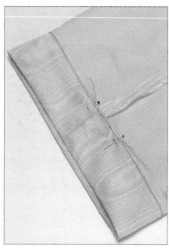

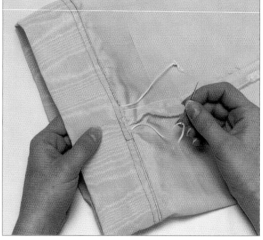

3 *Turn under one end to make a deep facing. Matching the seam, pin and stitch along the fold of the hem, leaving a gap at the seam.*

4 *Stitch a parallel seam 5/8 in (1.25 cm) away to make a narrow casing, but stitch across the seam without leaving a gap. Repeat steps 3 and 4 to make the casing at the other end of the tube.*

5 *Knot one end of a length of cord and thread it through the casing. Use a bodkin if a safety pin is too big. Knot the other end and pull the cord to gather. Thread a cord through the other casing, but do not pull up.*

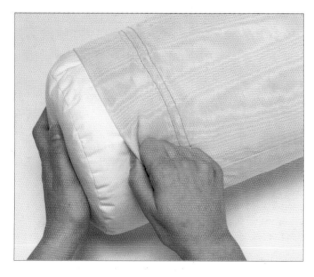

6 *Turn the cover right side out and insert the pad. Pull up the cord on the other end to gather and make a slipknot to secure.*

7 *The gathered ends can be short, as here, or longer. Face them with a contrasting fabric for added visual interest.*

Zipped Piped Bolster

1 Cut one piece of fabric to measure the length and circumference of the pad, plus a generous seam allowance all around. Cut two circles to measure the diameter of the pad end plus seams. Mark seamlines on all the pieces.

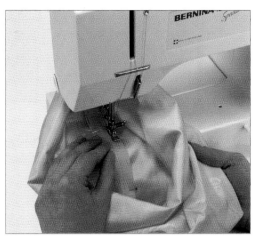

2 Fold the main piece of fabric in half lengthwise, with right sides together. Stitch each end up to the zipper position. Baste the seam closed and insert the zipper in the seam allowance on the wrong side (see page 76). Remove basting.

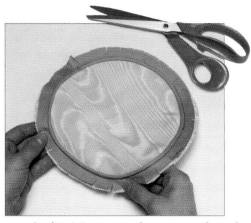

3 Apply piping, or another trim, to the end pieces (see pages 46 and 130). Clip the seam allowance all around each end piece; this will help ease the ends onto the main piece.

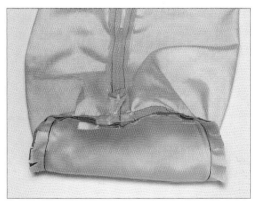

4 Clip into the seam allowances at the ends of the main piece. Open the zipper. With right sides together, pin, baste and stitch the end pieces to the main piece.

5 Turn the piped bolster cover right sides out through the open zipper. Insert the bolster pad and close.

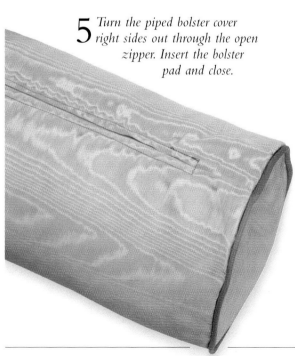

USEFUL TIP

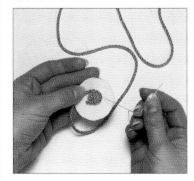

To make a medallion for bolster ends, cut a circle from heavy interfacing and baste the end of a decorative cord in the center. Wind the cord around in a spiral, catching it down with basting stitches. Attach a tassel through the center, if desired.

DECORATIVE IDEAS

Faced Gathered Bolster
Facings in a contrasting fabric have been sewn in as separate pieces at the ends. A wired ribbon in coordinating colors finishes the ends.

Pleated Ruffle Bolster
For this effect, apply a ruffled trim at each end of the tube. Add straight pieces and gather the ends, as for the tasselled bolster below. Attach buttons to cover.

Tasselled Bolster
Straight pieces have been sewn onto each end of the tube. Gathering stitches, sewn along the raw edges, were pulled up, tied off and covered with tassels (see Useful Tip, left).

Slipcovers

THE TECHNIQUE FOR making slip-on covers is basically the same for sofas and chairs. All the seams on the old cover can be opened and the pieces used as a pattern, or a pattern can be cut from inexpensive cotton lining, then basted together to check fit. Your fabric must be able to withstand wear and tear and not fray too readily. Match patterned fabric at crucial joining points, and position and center large motifs carefully. Allow extra fabric in these cases.

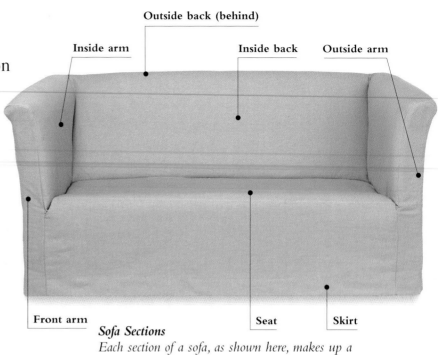

Sofa Sections
Each section of a sofa, as shown here, makes up a separate pattern piece and must be measured accurately.

Measuring a Sofa

To estimate how much fabric you need, measure each section lengthwise at longest point, then widthwise at widest point. Add 4 in (10 cm) to all measurements for seam allowances and hems, and 8 in (20 cm) for edges to be tucked in. To make the cover easy to take on and off, an overlap opening can be made in the center back, or fasteners such as buttons, ties and popper snap tape can be used along the back and the outside arm edges. Allow extra fabric 4 in (10 cm) for center-back overlap and 6 in (15 cm) for side openings. Zippers must be heavy-duty and suitable for the fabric weight. For patterned fabric, allow extra fabric for fitting. Include separate seat cushions (see pages 138–41) and armcovers (see page 149) in the calculations.

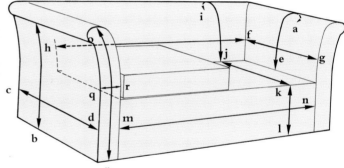

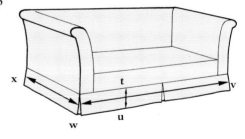

Arm Sections (left)

The outside arm measurement begins at the seam joining the inside arm piece to the outside. Note that the inside arm section (a–e) curves over the top of the arm. The front arm (o–p) is a gusset which joins the inside and outside arm sections. On box-shaped sofas and armchairs, the gusset extends over the top of the arm, with both inside and outside arm sections attached along two sides.

Sofa Back (right)

The lengthwise measurement (c–c) is taken across the widest point on the back of the sofa. The height measurement (i–s) extends from the top seam to the floor.

Skirt (above)

The skirt, sometimes called the apron, generally hangs from the front edge of the seat to the floor (k–l), but it can also be a separate strip (t–u) joined at the bottom of the seat overhang and reaching to the floor. This strip can extend just along the front of the sofa (v–w) or it can cover the same depth at the sides (w–x) and even the back, if desired. Skirts can be pleated or box-pleated, which requires extra fabric.

Measuring a Chair

A slipcover can be made for any type of chair or stool, from a large overstuffed armchair to an upright wooden-backed kitchen chair. Covers for chairs with arms are measured and constructed like sofa covers, or made without the arm sections (see pages 150–1). Upright chairs without arms and stools can be covered with a full skirt; such chairs can also be lightly padded, and the backs as well as the seats covered. Generally, the sections that make up a chair cover are the seat, skirt, backrest and back. The side section, or gusset, can be made as a separate piece or cut out as part of the backrest.

Crucial Measurements

Sofa

a–b	height of outside arm
c–d	width of outside arm
a–e	length of inside arm
f–g	width of inside arm
h–f	length of inside back
i–j	height of inside back
j–k	depth of seat
k–l	depth of skirt
m–n	length of seat and skirt
o–p	height of front arm gusset
q–r	width of front arm gusset
c–c	length of outside back
i–s	height of outside back
t–u	depth of separate skirt
v–w	length of separate skirt (front)
w–x	length of separate skirt (sides)

Chair

a–b	height of backrest
c–d	width of backrest
b–e	depth of seat
f–g	width of seat
e–h	depth of seat
f–h	height of seat
i–i	width between front legs
i–j	width between front and back legs
k–l	height of gusset from top of backrest to arm
m–n	height of gusset from arm to bottom of seat
o–c	width of side gusset
p–q	depth of skirt
r–s	height of back
t–u	height of back with skirt
v–w	width of back

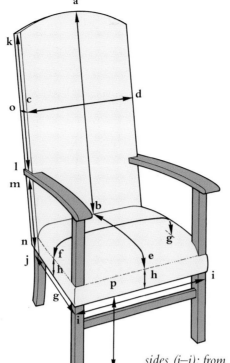

Chair Front
Mark the crucial measurements of each section on a rough sketch: backrest height (a–b) and width (c–d); seat depth (b–e), width (f–g) and height (e–h and f–h); from corners of legs across front (i–i), back and sides (i–j); from top of backrest to arm (k–l), from bottom of arm to back leg (m–n), across the width of the side gusset (o–c). If you are making a cover with a full skirt, add the measurement from the seat to the floor (p–q).

Chair Back
Measure the back of the chair at the highest point from the top to the bottom (r–s), or to the floor (t–u) if making a full skirt, and across the width at the widest point (v–w).

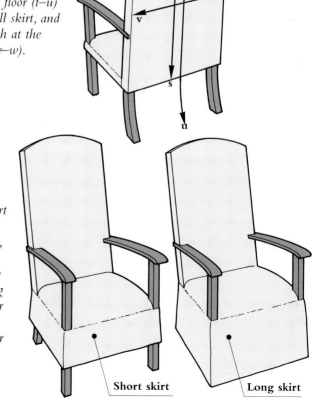

Skirt Lengths
Some chairs lend themselves to a full skirt. A slightly gathered or pleated skirt reaching to the floor creates a romantic look, while a shorter skirt looks more tailored. Be careful when measuring to get the scale right, or the chair may look badly proportioned. For a more upholstered finish, see the fitted cover on pages 150–1.

Short skirt   **Long skirt**

SOFA COVERS

Making a loose slipcover for a sofa may appear to be a daunting task at first. Some basic sewing skills and a good-sized working area are necessary, but if you follow the steps given here, covering a sofa or an armchair should be a straightforward project that can save money. The secret is to make an under-cover from inexpensive cotton lining, which can be cut and marked, stitched together to check the fit, and then used as a pattern for cutting out the cover from the main fabric.

Making a Fabric Pattern

1 Measure the sofa as described on page 144, allowing for a center-back opening. Roughly, but generously, cut one outside arm section from inexpensive cotton lining fabric.

2 Using extra-long dressmaker's pins, pin the cut piece all around in position on the outside arm of the sofa.

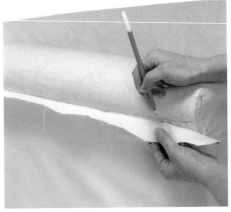

3 Mark the seamline all around the pinned piece. The marks can be rough at this stage, but must be clear. A water-soluble marker has been used here. Cut, pin and mark another identical piece of fabric for the other outside arm section.

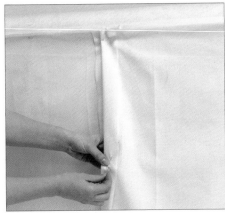

4 Roughly cut out the back section in two pieces from the cotton fabric, allowing for an overlap. Pin the first back piece in place on the sofa. Turn back and pin the center fold, then repeat for the second half of the back section.

5 Mark all back seamlines on the two pieces. Mark the center fold carefully on the piece that will overlap the other.

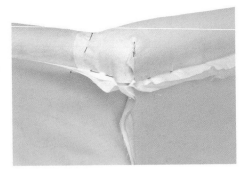

6 Roughly cut out one inside arm section from the cotton fabric, cutting generously to allow for the tuck-ins and shaping around corners. Pin in place on the sofa. Cut a dart as necessary to make the corner fit and ease the fabric. Repin until the corner and outside arm section fit together snugly.

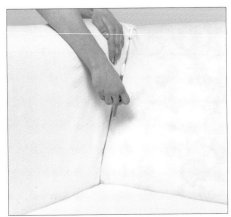

7 Smooth the inside arm section, tucking it into the corners, and mark the seamlines. Mark clearly inside the tuck-in.

8 Slash into seam allowance in the top inside corner as necessary to ease the tension, then mark the corner. Repeat steps 6–8 to make the other inside arm section.

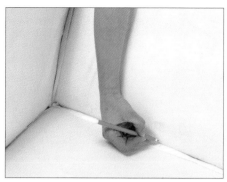

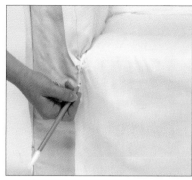

9 Cut out the inside back section from the cotton fabric and pin in place on the sofa. Smooth the fabric and tuck in the edges where the inside back meets the seat. Mark the seamlines, pushing the marking pen into the tight corners as necessary.

10 Cut the seat and front skirt as one section from the cotton fabric. Starting at the point where the seat meets the inside back, smooth the fabric toward the front, pressing and tucking into the corners on all three sides.

11 Roughly cut a narrow front arm gusset from the cotton fabric. Inset: Pin it in place on the sofa to join the inside and outside arm sections, starting at the top of the curve. Then pin the seam along both long edges so the front arm section is pinned to the outside arm, inside arm and skirt sections. Repeat for the other front arm.

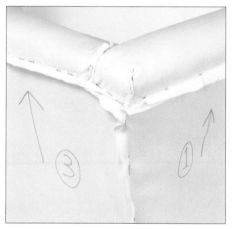

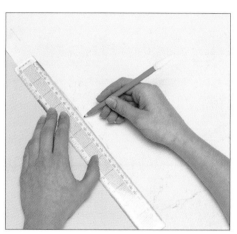

12 Mark each section with numbers or letters to identify them; for example, mark a 1 on both outside arm pieces, a 2 on both inside arm sections, and so on. Draw arrows to indicate the top of each section.

13 Unpin all the sections. Lay each one flat and straighten the seamline markings using the water-soluble marker.

Checking the Fit

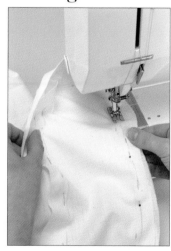

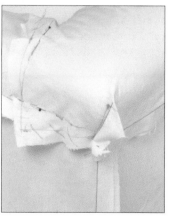

1 Working in the same order as steps 1–11 of making a fabric pattern, machine-stitch the entire cover together along the marked seamlines. Use a loose basting stitch that can be unpicked easily.

2 Put the basted slipcover, wrong side out, on the sofa. Drape the arms loosely first, then work from front to back, smoothing the fabric down carefully to cover the entire sofa.

3 Where the fit is not perfect, re-mark the seams, drawing dashes through old marked lines as shown. Repin along the new seamlines. Remove the cover and, unpicking where necessary, machine-baste along the new seamlines.

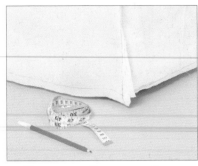

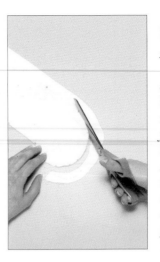

4 *Repeat step 2 to try on the restitched cover. If necessary, repeat step 3. When you are satisfied with the fit, measure and mark the bottom hemline all around.*

5 *Making sure that all the identifying marks are still visible, unpick the entire cover. Press each section flat, but do not use a steam iron because the steam will remove the pen marks.*

6 *Trim each section carefully along the seamline, as shown. A generous seam allowance will need to be added to each piece when cutting out the final sofa cover from the main fabric. Alternatively, retain the seam allowance to make an under-cover from the fabric pattern (see Useful Tip, below left).*

USEFUL TIP

To use the fabric pattern pieces as a protective under-cover for the sofa, trim pieces with seam allowances included. The seam allowances can be pinned back and the pieces used to cut out the pattern from the main fabric to make the outer slipcover.

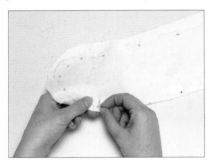

1 *For each fabric pattern piece, fold the seam allowance under and pin in place along the seamline. Pin onto the wrong side of the main fabric, as in step 1 of Finishing the Slipcover, and trace around each piece.*

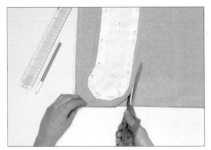

2 *Draw outline for seam allowance around each piece and cut out. When the fabric pattern pieces are unpinned, the seamlines on each main fabric piece will provide a guideline along which to stitch.*

Finishing the Slipcover

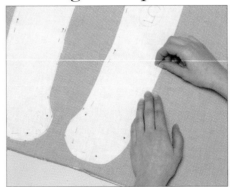

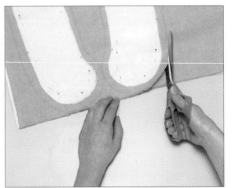

1 *Using the trimmed sections as the pattern, pin onto the wrong side of the main fabric, making sure enough fabric is left all around each section for seam allowances. Check that they are the right way up and that you have all the right- and left-hand pieces where needed. Match fabric patterns carefully, if necessary.*

2 *Mark around each pattern piece, including a seam allowance of about 1/2 in (1.25 cm) all around, and transfer all the identifying marks. Cut the pieces out and machine-stitch the sections together, working in the same order as steps 1–11 of Making a Fabric Pattern (see pages 146–7).*

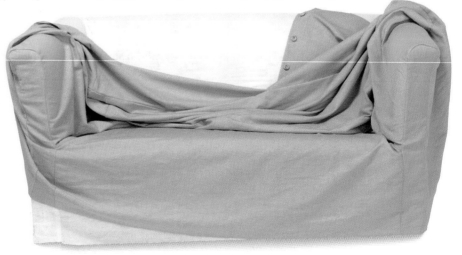

3 *Put the finished cover on the sofa from front to back. Check the fit, then mark and hand-sew the bottom hem all around.*

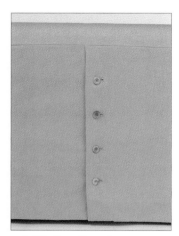

4 *Mark and work buttonholes (see pages 78–9) in the overlap piece at the center back and sew corresponding buttons on the underlap section. Alternatively, you can use matching ties or other fastenings.*

5 *The finished sofa looks inviting and stylish with armcovers (see below), seat cushions (see pages 138–9) and scatter cushions (see pages 130–5).*

Armcovers

Armcovers provide a practical way of protecting the surface of the arms of a chair or sofa. They can be removed and cleaned separately, and they provide an extra layer to help guard against everyday wear and tear on the vulnerable top of the arms.

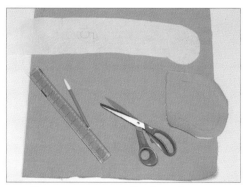

1 *Cut out two rectangles from the main fabric, each measuring as the inside arm of the sofa (a–e x f–g). Cut out two front arm pieces from the main fabric using the pattern of the front arm sections, but only to a depth of o–e, plus hems (see page 144).*

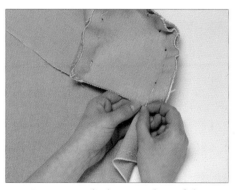

2 *Zigzag-stitch the raw edges of the arm front pieces. Pin and baste one front arm piece to one rectangle, starting at one straight edge of the rectangle as shown. Repeat to make a piece that is a mirror image. Stitch both along the basting.*

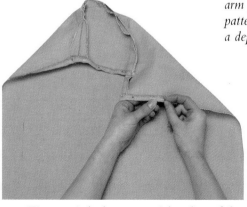

3 *Zigzag-stitch the raw straight edges of the rectangular pieces. Turn under and pin a hem along zigzagged edges on both armcovers. Pin open the seam on the short edge and fold out the seam on the long side as shown.*

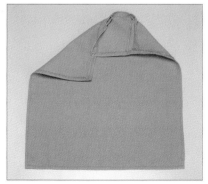

4 *Starting at the long front corner on one armcover, stitch a single hem all around, turning the corners neatly. Repeat on the other armcover.*

5 *The finished armcovers fit smoothly and snugly over the arms of the sofa, protecting the surface.*

CHAIR COVER

The chair shown here is a Victorian upright chair with pretty detailing on the wooden arms. A cover could have been made with arms, in the same way as the sofa cover on pages 146–9, but it seemed a shame to hide the chair arms, so the original cover was removed and used as a fabric pattern instead of cutting a pattern from inexpensive cotton.

The original cover for this chair consists of: a seat piece (h x g plus an underlap of 3 in/7.5 cm on the front and sides); a backrest piece (a-b x c-d plus o-c on the top and sides); and a back piece (r-s x v-w plus an underlap of 3 in/7.5 cm on the bottom edge). Tabs with popper-snap tape sewn to them were used to secure the cover. Fabric-tape loops were added along the bottom edge of seat and back pieces, and tape threaded through the loops to secure the cover underneath the chair.

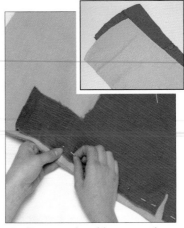
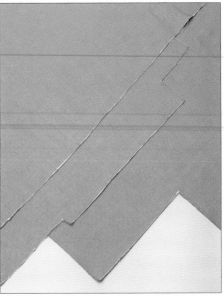

1 *Remove the old cover and unpick all the seams carefully. Press the pieces and use them to cut out a new piece for each old one. Work carefully to prevent fraying on the old pieces. Make sure all darts, flaps, and other markings are transferred to each piece. Inset: Using the old pieces for guidance, mark the seamlines on each new piece.*

2 *Mark all tabs, positions for armholes and back uprights, and all other features carefully. Shown here are the bottom corner of the back piece (top), the front corner of the seat (middle), and the armhole on the backrest (bottom).*

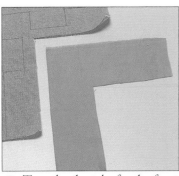

FACINGS

Facings on slipcovers finish the edges and carry ties or fasteners.

3 *To make the tabs for the front seat corner, cut a generous facing from medium-weight dress fabric, as shown in step 1 of Facings (right). It should be shaped to fit – this is L-shaped.*

4 *Pin facing to fabric, right sides together, and stitch along marked seamline. Cut away up to seam allowance and clip corners. Turn facing to wrong side to enclose raw edges. Stitch the folded facing in place, as shown in step 2 of Facings. Repeat for the other front corner and try it on the chair to check the fit.*

1 *Mark seamline on main fabric. Cut a piece of medium-weight coordinating lining fabric, larger than area to be cut away. Pin and stitch along seamline right sides together. Cut away excess and clip corners.*

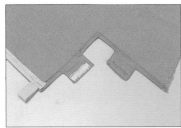

5 *At each corner, sew popper-snap tape to the wrong, faced, side and a corresponding length to the right side of the tab. Pin and stitch a length of loop tape (see opposite) to the front and side raw edges.*

6 *The lower section of the back piece is not stitched to the backrest piece, but is faced below the arms and joined with popper-snap tape. First face the corners neatly (see left). With right sides together, pin facing to the back piece at the bottom corner and stitch. Snip away a triangular piece of main fabric below the armhole to make a neat turning.*

2 *Turn facing to wrong side of fabric to enclose raw edges. Pin and topstitch. Inset: Sitching appears on right side; facing on wrong side.*

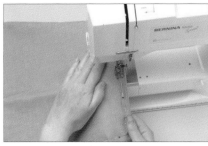

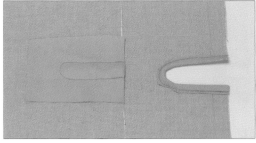

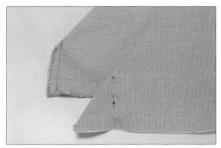

7 To finish the back piece facing, fold the facing strip to the wrong side. Trim and snip as required by the shape of the seam. Pin the facing in place and topstitch (see Facings, opposite).

8 For backrest armhole facings, cut two rectangles at least 2 in (5 cm) larger than armhole. Pin and stitch to cover armhole position on each side. Turn under a single hem, below armholes. Pin and stitch on each side.

9 Make darts at the top corners of the backrest piece so the cover fits neatly over them. Fold each corner to the required depth and pin it in place. Stitch the seam, trim the corner and zigzag edges together. With right sides together, pin and stitch back and backrest pieces together along top and down each side to armholes.

10 With the seat piece in place, try the assembled back piece on the chair. Adjust to make sure the pieces fit along the back seat seam and clip corners as necessary. Remove the two pieces and zigzag all seam edges to finish them. If desired, try the pieces on the chair again and make any further adjustments.

11 Pin and stitch raw inside edge of seat piece to raw bottom edge of backrest. Try for fit. When satisfied, remove and pin and stitch popper-snap tape on each single hem below the armholes on the backrest. Stitch corresponding tape to each facing on back piece. Zigzag seams.

12 Put the cover on the chair again and check the length of the back piece for positioning the tape loops along the bottom edge. Remove the cover. Pin and stitch the tape loops in position (see Tape Loops, right). Try the cover on again.

TAPE LOOPS

Lengths of tape with loops attached can be applied to edges of covers that can be pulled tight to create a smooth, upholstered look.

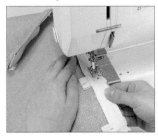

1 Cut tape to required length plus 1 in (2.5 cm). Cut a 2-in (5-cm) piece of tape for each loop. Fold loop pieces in half and pin. Pin and stitch to raw edge of cover on right side. Stitch in place, folding up short ends.

14 The finished cover fits snugly and smoothly. This technique can be used to cover chairs without arms, in which case tabs do not need to be made for the armhole positions.

2 Turn the length of tape to wrong side of the cover, leaving the loops along the edge. Pin and stitch the unsewn tape edge along the length to secure it to the cover.

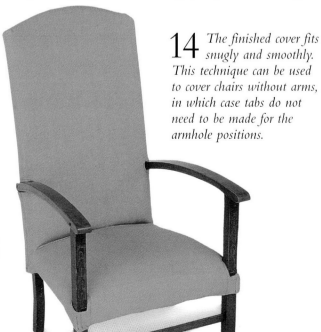

13 Turn the chair over and lace tape through the loops to pull the cover tightly.

CARE AND REPAIR

Although looking after clothes and furnishings usually seems second nature to most of us, especially if we have lavished time and attention on making them, proper informed care can greatly extend the life of fabric items. This chapter covers mending, stain removal, and laundry and cleaning information to help you care for your favorite things.

Care and Repair

TAKING PROPER CARE of home-made or purchased garments and furnishings keeps the items looking good. Mending a small tear means a favorite piece of clothing can be worn again, and the repair can usually be done so that it will be unnoticeable. Along with techniques for darning holes and restitching torn areas, there is useful information on laundering and stain removal in this chapter.

Darning a Hole in Wool

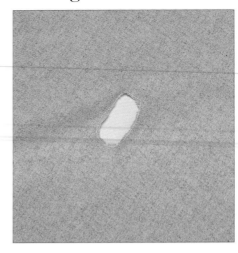

1 *To darn a small hole in a wool skirt or suit, trim around the hole to neaten the edges. Zigzag-stitch all around the shape, close to the edge.*

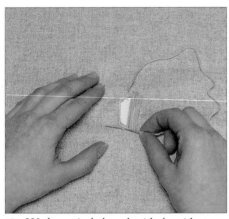

2 *Work vertical threads side by side to cover the hole completely. Use a thread that matches the fabric in both color and weight – here a large needle and heavy thread have been used for clarity.*

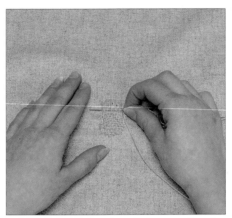

3 *Work crosswise threads by weaving the thread in and out of the vertical threads, keeping each row as close to the previous one as possible and working from side to side. To begin each new row, stitch over the edge of the hole.*

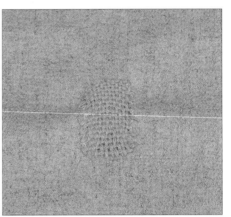

4 *The finished darn will be virtually invisible if it is worked in a thread that closely matches the color and weight of the garment itself. If you wish, you can unravel thread from a seam allowance or hem of the garment.*

Patching a Hole in Plaid Fabric

1 *Cut away the tear to form a square, following the pattern of the plaid. Cut out a new patch in the same fabric, larger all around than the hole and matching the plaid pattern of the garment.*

2 *Pin and stitch the right side of the patch to the wrong side of the garment. Use matching thread; a contrasting thread is used here for clarity. On the right side, clip halfway to the stitching at the corners.*

3 *Working on the right side, turn under each raw edge to the clipped corner and pin. Topstitch the turned-under edges in place. Again, be sure to use matching thread, not contrasting as here.*

4 *The finished patch blends beautifully into the pattern of the fabric. If stitched in an appropriately colored thread to match the lines of the plaid, it would be almost invisible.*

Ready-to-use Patches

Patches can be used to cover holes or worn areas to extend the life of a garment. Since they can be used only on the right side of the garment, they should be viewed as decorative repairs.

Ready-made Leather Patches

Sometimes available with prepunched holes, these can be sewn on by hand or machine to cover worn elbows on jackets or sweaters. Thin suede or leather can also be cut into shapes and used.

Iron-on Appliqué patches
Available in a wide choice of sizes, colors and designs, these patches can be used to cover a tear or stain, or simply to add a decorative effect. Follow the manufacturer's instructions carefully to apply.

Woven Patches
These patches, which are available both with and without an adhesive backing, can be stitched onto garments and furnishings. Those without adhesive are not as rigid as the iron-on variety.

Repairing a Torn Seam

1 *To mend a seam that is torn along the stitched seamline, cut a strip of iron-on mending fabric, available from fabric departments, slightly wider than the seam. Press it in place on the wrong side, over the torn area.*

2 *Working on the right side of the garment, stitch along each side of the torn seam to secure the mending fabric. Here the seam is shown from the wrong side. This method can be used to strengthen a seam where the stitching has come apart but the fabric is not torn.*

Repairing an Underarm Seam

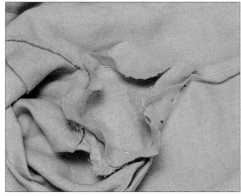

1 *Starting at the underarm point on the wrong side of the garment, unpick the seam in all four directions. Cut a bias square larger than the opened area from the same fabric. Pin, then baste it in place with right side down, so each edge of the square meets the bias of the garment from seam to seam.*

2 *Working carefully to avoid stretching the bias edges, stitch the patch along all four sides on the wrong side of the garment.*

3 *Working from the right side of the garment, topstitch around the edge of the patch to secure it further. Inset: Trim the edges of the finished square patch on the wrong side of the fabric to create a diamond-shaped underarm gusset.*

Repairing a Worn Buttonhole

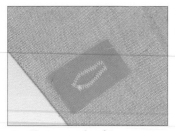

1 *Cut a patch of iron-on mending fabric to cover the torn area completely. Iron the patch to the wrong side of the garment over the tear. Zigzag-stitch around the buttonhole on the right side.*

2 *Using a seam ripper or a pair of small sharp scissors, slit through the mending fabric to open the buttonhole. Trim away any visible mending fabric.*

Repairing a Torn Button Band

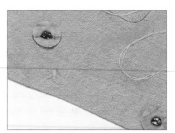

1 *Cut a generous patch of iron-on mending fabric to cover the tear. Iron it in place over the tear and work a small circle of tiny running stitches all around the torn area.*

2 *Sew a button in position, stitching through the mending fabric. The button will conceal the torn area and the mending fabric makes the area strong enough to stitch through.*

Ripping Seams

Most home-sewers will need to remove a row of stitching occasionally, to repair a torn seam for example, and here are two ways to accomplish this task.

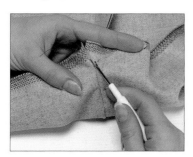

Using a Seam Ripper
Hold the seam open at one end and insert the seam ripper carefully between the first stitches. With a quick upward action, slice through the stitch to cut the thread, then move on to the next secured stitch. Cutting one stitch usually causes several stitches to unravel.

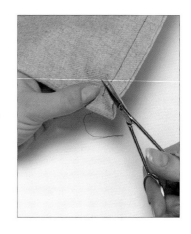

Using Scissors
To rip a seam open with small pointed scissors, lay the garment flat and insert the point of one scissors blade under a stitch. Cut the thread carefully, then repeat every 3–4 stitches. The seam then opens easily and the threads can be gently pulled out.

Fabric Care

Following the manufacturer's advice regarding the care and laundering of fabric will ensure that garments and furnishings last for a long time and keep their shape, texture and color.

A universal pictograph of symbols for fabric care is used by most countries. The major exception is the United States, where most care labels are printed with instructions in words. In both cases, a care label is sewn into a seam of ready-made clothes, and most fabric suppliers can provide care labels to be used by home-sewers and dressmakers.

Washing

Normal cycle at 140°F (60°C), normal spin

Normal cycle at 100°F (40°C), normal spin

Normal cycle at 85°F (30°C) or Gentle cycle, normal rinse, normal spin

Hand wash, maximum temperature 100°F (40°C)

Do not wash

Ironing

High – cotton/linen, 400°F (200°C)

Warm – polyester blends/wool 300°F (150°C)

Low – synthetics/silk 200°F (110°C)

Do not iron

Bleaching

Diluted cold chlorine bleach may be used

Do not use chlorine bleach

Any solvent except Trichlorethlene

Do not dry-clean

Tumble dry at high heat

Tumble dry at low heat

Do not tumble dry

Stain Removal

Perhaps the single most effective aspect of fabric care is the fast removal of stains. The chart here outlines methods for dealing with some common accidents.

Treat stains quickly. It is harder to remove most dry stains. Blot excess moisture away before treating and work on the wrong side of fabric if possible.

Some stain-removal products are formulated for specific stains. Always follow the manufacturer's instructions carefully, and test all cleaning solutions on a hidden area first. Apply chemical cleaning agents only to the stain itself, or it may spread. On large areas, work from the edges of the stain toward the middle.

Using the Chart

These treatments apply to washable fabrics. Stains on non-washable and delicate fabrics should be handled by a professional dry-cleaner. Look in the left-hand column for the stain to be treated.

Follow the numbers in sequence. Where numbers are repeated, choose the most convenient method. Repeat if necessary. Set the temperature and washing cycle specified on the garment label.

C = cold water
W = warm water
H = hot water
If no temperature symbol is given, follow the washing instructions for the garment.

Stain	Soak	Rinse	Wash	Blot	Harden by rubbing with an ice cube	Scrape	Pretreat with appropriate chemical before washing	Bleach (whites only)	Lemon	Salt	Press	Remarks
Adhesives and glue	4W		4		1	2	3					
Alcohol			1H									— 1 part white wine vinegar to 3 parts water if stain persists
Blood	1C						2					
Chewing gum			4		1	2	3					
Chocolate		1W					2					
Cosmetics							1					— Treat basically as grease
Egg							1					— Use enzyme (biological) washing powder
Grass							1	2				
Grease and oil			2H				1					
Ink			2H				1					— Washing may set the stain
Mildew			2H					1	1	1		— Mix lemon juice with salt and sun-dry
Milk			1									
Paint: water-based		1W	2									
Paint: oil-based			3	1			2					
Perspiration	1W		2									— Soak affected area in water with a spoonful of borax added
Rust			3W						1	2		— Mix lemon juice and salt and hold over steaming water
Scorch marks			1W						2	2		
Shoe polish						1	2					
Tea and coffee	1C						2					
Wax			3		1						2	
Wine and fruit juice	1		4	2			3			1		

INDEX

ACKNOWLEDGMENTS

There are a number of people without whom this book would not have been written: On the home front, David, who has always encouraged me even when he didn't understand my passion for stitching; and Daniel and Joshua, who uncomplainingly ate many oven-ready meals while I was overseeing photography and writing words. Doreen James, who stitched (almost) all of the samples, Lisa Dyer who made the words work and fit; Liz Brown who made the pictures fit and work; Matthew Ward, who took the superlative photographs, Sarah Hoggett, who persuaded me to do it, and Corinne Asghar, who made sure I did.